Planning and the Multi-local Urban Experience

The starting point of this book is the observation that there is a discrepancy between the lived reality of human beings and the fabricated, planned, and governed 'reality' of the state apparatus at both the local and national level.

The book posits multi-locality as an emerging spatial configuration. The author draws from various theoretical sources, such as Deleuze and Guattari's concepts of state or royal science, the Nietzschean critique of idealism, Hägerstrnad's time-geography, Hintikka's theory of modalities, Lefebvre's urban society, Castel's network society, Foucault's concept of heterotopia, and Bhaskar's and Satre's theories of presence and absence. He also discusses the implications of Faludi's post-territorialist critique of planning and governance, and of the failure to operationalise the concept quantitively, basing his arguments in the lived experiences of multi-locals as well.

The novelty of the book is how it analyses multi-locality from such a wide theoretical perspective: what is the nature and meaning of the different multiple and coexistent places for people, and how is this spatial transformation related to their mobility, everyday practices, and work. How does the presence and absence of places form their identity and their citizenship? He also addresses the inconsistency between multi-locality and traditional statistics and the planning and governance practices based on the assumption of unilocality and discusses the implications of this incongruity.

The book will be of interest to scholars in urban studies and planning theory, as well as practitioners developing more adequate practices replacing outdated ones.

Kimmo Lapintie is Professor of Urban and Regional Planning and Head of Research at the Department of Architecture, Aalto University, Finland.

Routledge Advances in Regional Economics, Science and Policy

Governing Cities
Asia's Urban Transformation
Edited by Kris Hartley, Glen Kuecker, Michael Waschak, Jun Jie Woo, and Charles Chao Rong Phua

Mental Health and Wellbeing in Rural Regions
International Perspectives
Edited by Sarah-Anne Munoz and Steve F. Bain

Family Business and Regional Development
Edited by Rodrigo Basco, Roger Stough and Lech Suwala

Outsourcing in European Emerging Economies
Territorial Embeddedness and Global Business Services
Łukasz Mamica

The Regional Economics of Technological Transformations
Industry 4.0 and Servitisation in European Regions
Roberta Capello and Camilla Lenzi

Managing Knowledge, Governing Society
Social Theory, Research Policy and Environmental Transition
Alain-Marc Rieu

The Economics of Sustainable Transformation
Edited by Anna Szelągowska and Aneta Pluta-Zaremba

Planning and the Multi-local Urban Experience
The Power of Lifescapes
Kimmo Lapintie

For more information about this series, please visit: www.routledge.com/series/RAIRESP

Planning and the Multi-local Urban Experience
The Power of Lifescapes

Kimmo Lapintie

Routledge
Taylor & Francis Group

LONDON AND NEW YORK

First published 2022
by Routledge
4 Park Square, Milton Park, Abingdon, Oxon OX14 4RN

and by Routledge
605 Third Avenue, New York, NY 10158

Routledge is an imprint of the Taylor & Francis Group, an informa business

© 2022 Kimmo Lapintie

The right of Kimmo Lapintie to be identified as author of this work has been asserted in accordance with sections 77 and 78 of the Copyright, Designs and Patents Act 1988.

British Library Cataloguing-in-Publication Data
A catalogue record for this book is available from the British Library

Library of Congress Cataloging-in-Publication Data
Names: Lapintie, Kimmo, author.
Title: Planning and the multi-local urban experience : the power of lifescapes / Kimmo Lapintie.
Description: Abingdon, Oxon ; New York, NY : Routledge, 2022. |
Series: Routledge advances in regional economics, science and policy |
Includes bibliographical references and index.
Identifiers: LCCN 2021052675 (print) | LCCN 2021052676 (ebook) |
ISBN 9780367644239 (hardback) | ISBN 9780367644222 (paperback) |
ISBN 9781003124443 (ebook)
Subjects: LCSH: City planning--Political aspects. |
Urbanization--Social aspects. | Migration, Internal. | City-states.
Classification: LCC HT166 .L376 2022 (print) |
LCC HT166 (ebook) | DDC 307.1/216--dc23/eng/20211105
LC record available at https://lccn.loc.gov/2021052675
LC ebook record available at https://lccn.loc.gov/2021052676

ISBN: 978-0-367-64423-9 (hbk)
ISBN: 978-0-367-64422-2 (pbk)
ISBN: 978-1-003-12444-3 (ebk)

DOI: 10.4324/9781003124443

Typeset in Sabon
by KnowledgeWorks Global Ltd.

Contents

Preface

In the spring 2020, while I was writing this book, the global pandemic from COVID-19 virus spread from China to Europe and the Americas, resulting in lockdowns adopted by national governments, including closing of national and even regional borders, curfews, and extreme disciplinary actions, such as closing services and restricting mobility in public spaces and large gatherings. As a result, cities and countries experienced a major economic shock, requiring bailouts from the governments.

Many people were ordered to work online, and even across national boundaries that had been closed from physical access. As a result, a major leap in digitalization occurred almost overnight. Schools and universities were also closed in many countries, and parents with small children had to accommodate to the demands of their children studying remotely. Some people moved to their second homes to work, but others had to find ways to change their (often small) homes into ad hoc offices and classrooms. Those who were used to travel to different homes in several countries were unable to cross national borders, which had been a substantial part of their normal life. Suddenly, multi-locality had come out from the marginal to become a 'new normal'. There is probably not going to be any return to the old normal: the employers have noticed that it makes no sense to pay for large office spaces if they are not used efficiently, and workers have also noticed the savings of their time and money earlier used for travelling, as well as an additional hour of sleep. They do miss their colleagues, but encounters don't necessarily mean sitting by the desk from nine to five. Work, life, and work-life are going through a major transformation.

Our conceptual and methodological framework, on the other hand—to say nothing of a theoretical insight—seems to be lagging behind. Most countries are still using methodologies that are not able to catch even the basic elements of the phenomenon of multi-locality. Additionally, concepts like workplace, home, second home, summer cottage, tourism, vacation apartments, work apartments, etc. seem to be outdated, as the borderlines between living and working have become blurred, and as the assumption that there has to be *one* home and *one* workplace, around which all the other places are *secondary*, is not self-evidently true any longer. As I will try to demonstrate in this book, many traditional conceptualizations of urbanisation, mobility, living, working, space, and place have genuine difficulties in dealing with multi-locality. The same is true of planning and governance, which both implicitly favour its opposite, unilocality.

Multi-locality as a phenomenon is not new, of course. People have for a long time been forced—or chosen—to work in another municipality or even in another country than where their family ties are. Conversely, people living in cities have fled to their second homes in the countryside, and some have lived in several homes in different countries. Nevertheless, several fundamental changes in society are together striving human spatiality to the direction of multi-locality.

The first of them is, of course, the development of information and communication technologies. If working from home or from places like libraries or coffee shops used to be possible only for very few workers (such as researchers, writers, artists, or interpreters), portable computers and wi-fi-networks have made it possible for all those whose work mainly deals with information.

Second, people are getting older. In 2018, the number of persons above 65 surpassed the number of children under 5, and in 2050 their number will be twice the number of children (United Nations, 2019, p. 16). Unlike small children and their parents, these people are mostly retired and are not tied to a physical workplace, city, or country. For retirees, concepts like work-time and leisure make no sense anymore, nor do the concepts derived from them (such as summer cottage, holiday resort, leisure apartment, work apartment, etc.). But this does not mean that they would simply choose one place of residence, according to their preferences. They may, for instance, spend more time in their 'second' homes than in their 'permanent' address, which again shows how artificial and outdated these concepts are.

Third, our work-life is undergoing major changes. The expertise required in most jobs is becoming more specialized, which implies the need to acquire higher education. This is one of the driving forces of urbanization, since higher education institutions such as universities tend to concentrate in major cities, as well as the businesses utilizing their spill-over effects. However, this also means that the specialized and highly educated couples don't necessarily find suitable jobs close to each other, despite the diversity of jobs in cities. If you want to build a successful career, you need to accept a good job offer when it is available. But what about your husband, wife or partner? Women no longer quit their jobs and follow their husbands, which means a complicated reorganization of family life: family members may live apart in two separate homes close to their workplaces, or they may choose a new place of residence in the middle, providing shorter distances to both. These challenges are highlighted by the growing precariousness of employment: it makes no sense to give up your place of residence for a job opportunity that may last for a few months or a year, particularly if you would not even get a small apartment in the city with the price of one-family house in the countryside or smaller town.

Families are also going through structural changes. Even for the registered marriages, 40–50 percent of them end up in divorce, and the probability of divorce is highest after three years of marriage. This also means that there are more and more under-aged children whose biological parents live in two different addresses. In a shared custody, the child may spend an equal amount of time in each parent's home, even if he or she would be formally registered in only one of them. Co-habitation is probably no safer than marriage in terms of breaking up. If the parents end up in new relationships, there may be his, hers and common children, and the number of homes can be even more than two.

Last but not the least: even if you would like to move to the city close to your workplace, the price level may be unaffordable to you. Usually, the central cities in urban regions attract investors, even those who buy apartments without any intention to rent them our ('buy to leave'). The lower-middle-class workers in the service sector need to find homes farther away, resulting in long-distance commuting or the need to rent a smaller work apartment close to their workplace but away from their families during the weekdays.

All these different types of multi-locality have been studied from different perspectives by scholars in different disciplines (Schier et al., 2015), but in general research on the topic is yet taking shape and getting attention. Some would like to see multi-locality studies to develop into a new research field, since existing disciplinary research usually highlights some aspects of it and ignores others. Multi-locality is a phenomenon that is very difficult to study quantitatively, since the actual whereabouts of people are usually not registered, and, thus, we cannot trust traditional statistical data. Some results can be reached indirectly; for instance, if we know the number of holiday homes, the average number of people using them, and the average number of nights spent in them and when, we can get a rough picture of the 'real' number of people living in a municipality, if also the seasonal residents are included. The opposite case of living in a certain location and renting a work-apartment in another is even more difficult to study. Combining existing registers (which are based on the assumption of only one place of residence) can hardly give us any reliable knowledge.

Furthermore, even if we would be able to detect the numbers of different types of multi-local people, this would not give us the meaning of these different places or the practices and rhythms combining them. This requires qualitative studies such as interviews. The fact that these cannot be generalized is not a problem as such, if we are aware of it and aim for an understanding of the different types multi-locality there are, not so much about their share in the population.

In my research teams in Aalto University, we have tried to address these problems in various ways. Together with my former post-doctoral researcher Mina di Marino, we first started studying people who were working in non-traditional places such as libraries and coffee shops, by 'catching them in the act' and interviewing them (Di Marino & Lapintie, 2015). It was not difficult to find them, and it appeared that many of them used to work in several places during a single day—a good example of how impossible it is to follow multi-locals along their path through the city throughout the day. We also took a closer look at differences of libraries and coffee shops as parts of what we called post-functional city—the city where appropriation of places for activities not originally designed there have to be taken into account (Di Marino & Lapintie, 2017). In a subsequent project and together with my other post-doctoral researcher Johanna Lilius, we also regarded the phenomenon from the point of view of employers whose employees have the possibility to combine different places in their daily and weekly working practices (Di Marino et al., 2018).

However, this phenomenon also calls for theoretical understanding, something that we still seem to be lacking. It became evident, at least to me, that without questioning the conceptual framework of multi-locality studies we could tacitly adopt assumptions that are actually behind the common confusions around these new types of spatiality. This is quite obvious in the continuous attempts to study multi-locality with national statistics, which clearly do not reflect it. But one may also ask whether the questions we ask, such as the number of multi-locals and different types of them, are leading us astray. The chosen practices of people using different places are, namely, infinitely different, and trying to pigeon-hole them in abstract typologies is recreating the problems of statistics, only in a new guise. Many of the established concepts tacitly assume that there is a norm of living in only one place, and that multi-local practices represent 'otherness' that has to be explained and justified. These reflections lead us to the basic philosophical questions of the ontology and epistemology of multi-locality and, through them, to the ethical and political meanings of this emerging spatial configuration.

This book is my attempt to address these theoretical questions. Thus, my intention is not to provide a review of the growing theoretical and empirical literature on multi-locality, nor to list the different types of multi-locality, old and new (for such reviews, see e.g. Schier et al., 2015; Weiske et al., 2015). Neither is my intention to build a systematic theoretical construction of the phenomenon—it is too early for that. Rather I shall use multi-locality as a touchstone to assess the feasibility of different theoretical and conceptual frameworks on place, space, home, work, and urbanization in the light of this problem. I shall try to demonstrate that there are theoretical challenges related to it, and that they justify seeing multi-locality not as a specific phenomenon, but rather as an alternative perspective to old issues and problems.

Although my initial intention was to study and theorise multi-locality, in the end it became a sort of 'Wittgenstein's ladder' (Wittgenstein, 1922, statement 6.54) to be thrown out after having climbed on it to a new understanding of human spatiality as *lifescapes*. Like landscapes, lifescapes determine the potentiality and power of corporeal human beings, as potential mobility in places and regions open to them.

1 Introduction

Revealing the paradox

The pandemic of 2020–22 did not only make life difficult but was also an interesting 'reality check' of our current ways of conceptualizing the city, mobility, and urbanization. Almost overnight, the dominant narrative of urbanization was turned upside down—or, to be more exact, it revealed itself as a narrative. Suddenly, all of the features that were part of the success story of cities—size, density, diversity, connectedness—also became part of their vulnerability. The compact city became the contagious city, and the Utopian urbanism faced a pandemic dystopia. It is actually interesting that such a Utopian narrative could develop in the contemporary world, which has rather been characterized by dystopian stories, such as nuclear war or climate change.

Consider the title of one of the most famous books of neo-liberal urbanism, Edward Glaeser's 'Triumph of the City: How Our Greatest Invention Makes Us Richer, Smarter, Greener, Healthier, and Happier' (Glaeser, 2011). It does not only sound rather naïve in the light of recent events but also shows the main features of the urban narrative. But if the city has triumphed, who was the enemy? The countryside? Historically, this could make some sense: the bourgeois city did indeed triumph over the feudal system of large estates in the countryside. But more recently? Hasn't the countryside been the weaker party ever since the industrial revolution? But perhaps the enemy is the nation state? There has indeed been a lot of pre-pandemic talk of 'hollowing out' or even 'dismantling' of the nation state, also by scholars of urban studies (Holliday, 2002).

For local politicians, the idea is alluring. For instance, in 2018 the Mayor of Helsinki declared, in a glossy leaflet, that 'the city is the new state'. It turned out to be a premature declaration of victory. Clearly, it was the nation state that could adopt such hard measures as closing the borders or declaring curfews. The nation states still have the monopoly of legitimate use of force, and they are also ready to use it: the police and the armed forces enforced the lockdowns all over the world. This is something that cities could not have done, in spite of their image as engines of local and global economies.

DOI: 10.4324/9781003124443-1

Nevertheless, if we try to understand the 'triumph' as part of the urban narrative, we need to find an enemy. There needs to be fighting and hardships before the victory can be declared. The main character is usually sent on a journey and comes out as a different person after a series of difficulties and dangers. Correspondingly, the early industrial city with its unhealthy environment and social injustice, the problems famously described by Engels in his 1844 book on the Condition of the Working Class in England (Engels, 2005), can be seen as the enemy—in fact many popular stories do describe industrialization and the exploitation of both people and the environment as such an enemy. The triumph of the city would in that case mean solving these problems with better sanitation, better urban design, and the welfare state, since the socialist Utopias promoted by Engels have been out of fashion for some time. Some of these are also discussed by Glaeser, particularly clean water, but good urban design and strong welfare state are excluded from his Utopia. I shall return to his arguments later.

How could the urban narrative get such a dominant position in urban planning and politics, at the same time as the equally strong dystopian narrative of climate change prevailed? It was possible by arguing that the compact city is also an ecological city: shorter distances mean more pedestrians and cyclists, more public transport, and less car use. Less floor space per person means decreased CO_2 emissions from heating. The compact city is thus a win-win, a silver bullet, offering *both* economic growth through agglomeration effects *and* less CO_2 emissions and car-dependence. Peter Newman and Jeffrey Kenworthy became famous for their comparison of cities around the world, arguing that dense cities are less dependent on private cars and therefore more sustainable (Newman & Kenworthy, 1989). The argument was selective, however, since most of the other elements of sustainability were disregarded, such as higher consumption levels in cities, large peri-urban settlements around the compact and dense urban cores, and global flows of people, goods, and materials between cities.

Despite this, the urban narrative is persuasive for planners and politicians alike, and it is possible to build political coalitions around such a vision. As the planners of the city of Helsinki described it in their 'Vision 2050' from 2013:

> The theme pertaining to urbanism and urban culture depicts Helsinki in 2050 as a markedly more dense, ecological and vibrant metropolis. According to the attractive living theme, Helsinki is a socially balanced, dense and functionally versatile city, in which homes, workplaces, schools and services are close to one another and can be accessed easily. All everyday services are within walking or bicycling distance.
>
> (Helsinki City Plan, 2013, p. 5)

The keyword is, thus, density and its positive effects on urban life. The dystopian narrative of climate change is no counter-narrative, since the problem seems to be solved by compaction, even though it is a very slow policy option considering the urgency of mitigating climate change. But the pandemic narrative is entirely different: it hit at the heart of urbanization, and it did it very fast. Most people around the world faced its effects in a couple of months, which were not only health-related but also economic and social. It is, thus, a genuine counter-narrative, and as such it also revealed the urban narrative for what it is: a story and a Utopia.

However, this is not how urbanization and its problems are usually described. Many scholars within and around urban studies do not feel comfortable with concepts like narrative, which have their origin in literary theory and cultural studies. They want to be truth-tellers, not story-tellers. This is fair, but one may still ask whether urban studies and planning theory have benefitted enough from the textual or *discursive turn* that has proved to be useful in many social sciences and philosophy. Without necessarily committing oneself to the philosophies behind this turn, it makes sense to ask how words—and images—are in fact used in urban planning and politics. The fact that we are 'doing things with words' (Austin, 1962, p. 5) is, namely, self-evident already from the semantic point of view: when I say 'I promise', I am usually promising, not describing what I am doing.

Similarly, it is perhaps not enough to consider the 'truth' of stories like the urban or the pandemic narrative. They contain elements of truth, of course: cities do generate economic benefits and urban culture, but the possibility of pandemics resulting from density and connectedness is also a fact. Analysing them as narratives, in contrast, will make it possible to understand their selectivity and functions. Utopias clearly have different functions than Dystopias: the former are used to raise our spirit and lead us to a selected future scenario, while the latter are warning signs, kind of whistle blowing.

Narrative is, however, only one of the key concepts in the discursive turn, and it is often used rather loosely, embracing all kinds of meaningful linguistic elements. For instance, Emery Roe has developed an important theory and methodology of 'narrative policy analysis' (Roe, 1994), but he collected stories, scenarios, and arguments under the same concept of narrative. I would rather suggest that these different textual entities are analysed separately, since there are different methods and theories available for each of them. The implicit narratives or even 'grand narratives' told by 'truth-tellers' or 'serious speakers' as Foucault called them (Foucault, 1985b), are different from the openly constructed scenarios in futures studies, or the deliberately and painstakingly constructed arguments by which truth-claims are justified with evidence or reasoning in rational debates (Van Eemeren et al., 1996). And if the word 'argument' is taken in the sense that Perelman and Olbrechts-Tyteca gave it (Perelman & Olbrechts-Tyteca, 1971), we also have the whole tradition of rhetoric at our disposal. These subfields are connected, for sure, but the connections are an interesting topic of research as such. There is a rich variety of methods and theoretical perspectives which can be taken to use, as soon as we get rid of the tacit assumption that there is an 'invisible' language telling us only what the cities and urbanization 'really' are.

The obvious counter-argument for such a discursive approach is that we would lose touch with the concrete reality of cities, their social, economic, and technical aspects. Actually, the opposite is the case, as I try to demonstrate: conceptual analysis will lead us directly into the corporeal existence of citizens and their activities, something that official statistics, routinely used in urban studies, can never reach. Thereby, we can develop a critique of both the ontology (the 'reality') and the epistemology (our established ways of constructing knowledge) of mainstream planning, politics, and urban studies.

In the 2010s, innumerable publications of planning and urban studies have started with the claim that more than half of the world's population now lives in urban areas (e.g. Birch & Wachter, 2011; Shaw, 2018). According to the World Urbanization Prospects reports published yearly by the Population Division of the UN Department of Economic and Social Affairs, figures have shown that urbanization has continued: in the 2018 revision the share of the urban population was already 55% (United Nations, 2019). Interestingly, however, the authors using this reference never pause to ask the key question: what do we mean by 'live'? Even if the earth's surface could be divided into two exclusive forms of land-use, urban and non-urban—in which case the urban would, however, be in the minority—what does it mean to say that *people* are either urban or non-urban? Naturally, these results are arrived at by combining national censuses and population registers, but before a closer look at them, let us first dive from the globe to the level of an individual human being.

Let us consider a man who has rented a small apartment at the centre of the city. In the morning, he takes the metro to the neighbouring city where he works at a university. After work, he usually buys some groceries from the local shop and perhaps meets his friends at a local restaurant, or sometimes goes to the movies. He can also decide not to go to the office but work with his laptop in a library or in one of the several coffee shops in the area. He uses his apartment mostly for watching the TV and sleeping.

The elements of his daily life, thus, seem to be very urban. He prefers the city centre for its urban buzz and services within walking distance: restaurants, theatres, libraries, coffee shops, museums, shops, and department stores. For this reason, he is ready to accept a smaller apartment without balcony, as well as the noise and poor air quality typical of busy streets. He belongs to the educated workforce of universities, which is an essential resource of successful cities, helping information-intensive businesses to thrive. He sleeps and works in two different cities, as many people do in metropolitan areas. He uses public transport to get from his apartment to the university campus and to other locations. Thus, we should expect him to be one of the 'urbanites' who, according to the United Nations (UN), comprise more than half of the world's population. The only problem is that he does *not* live in the city. Is he dead then? A ghost?

Something less supernatural: every Friday, he takes his car and drives 200 kilometres to his villa in a rural municipality, where he spends his weekend with his wife. There he enjoys tending his garden, picking berries and mushrooms, or taking his boat to visit the nearby islands. The air is fresh and the sound of silence soothing. He may also extend the weekend and telework on Mondays and Fridays, giving his lectures and meeting his colleagues from Tuesdays to Thursdays. In this way, he gets the best of both worlds. In a word, he is *both* urban *and* rural, a *multi-local* resident.

However, the national legislation of his country and the corresponding population register only allow *one* permanent place of residence. In case he has two addresses where he actually *lives* as a corporeal human being (i.e. sleeps, cooks, watches the TV, etc.), he has to choose one of them as his 'proper' place of residence. It is called 'permanent residence' in statistics but, for him, both of the addresses are permanent (as much as any address can be permanent for mortal human beings). In addition to his own preference, the criteria accepted by the authorities for such 'proper' living are, for instance, work or family relationships. As he works in one city and his family lives in another, he can freely choose, probably optimizing his local taxation. Together with his wife, he has chosen the rural municipality as his 'permanent' residence. This is why he does not 'live' in the city, and thereby he is not included in the UN calculation of people who 'live in urban areas'. In the city, he is indeed a living dead, a ghost, in that sense.

One might be tempted to try and solve this paradox by saying that there are simply two senses of the word 'living', one referring to being alive, as a corporeal human being, and the other referring to being registered as a statistical unit. This homonymy is not restricted to the English language only: the Italian *vivere*, the German *Leben*, the Swedish *leva*, the Russian жить, and the Spanish *vivir* can all refer to being alive or residing. Contemporary Finnish is an exception to this rule, since the word *elää* can only be used for being alive, while *asua* means residing. But the situation is more complicated than this, which can clearly be seen in the methodology of population statistics. This is how the UN describes the role of population statistics in politics, planning, and urban development:

> With the increasingly potent data-processing power available to users of statistics, it is becoming critical to ensure that census data are exploited as comprehensively as possible. Detailed small-area statistics are imposing themselves as irreplaceable in pointing to the segments of everyday life that need to be improved in terms of living conditions, access to services, adequate infrastructure and fulfilment of essential human rights, such as the right to be registered or the right to vote.
>
> (United Nations, 2017)

'Everyday life' is, however, hardly the life that the statistical units are living, but rather the corporeal human beings, the living minds and bodies. One might suppose that it is *their* living conditions that should be improved, and that *they* are the ones who should be provided with the services. It is the corporeal human being who needs health care, it is the mind-body of his children who need to be able to go to school. The right to be registered or vote are partly corporeal rights: only those with a live body can vote, but one may have a body all right but not the right to vote. Thus, it seems that the methodology recommendations by the UN are strangely confusing these two entities, the corporeal human being and the statistical unit, the registered person. This is highlighted in the expressed need to gather 'detailed small-area statistics' that would guide our investments in services and infrastructure and also planning. The smaller the scale, however, the less probable it is that the corporeal human being is located in this small area confined by the statistician, at any given time. If we go to the smallest scale that the recommendation refers to—the individual address—it is most probable that the corporeal human being is not found there. He is living his everyday life mostly somewhere else.

Reflections like this have always made me feel uneasy. Why is it that some distinctions (such as the essential difference between living and staying) are quite natural to me, but they are often conflated or ignored in much of the literature written in English. Now, as I am also writing in English, which is not my native language, I need to be careful not to lose these distinctions with such concepts as living, man, population, growth, citizen, etc. While I was writing this book, I came up with a newspaper article on the Estonian author Jaan Kaplinski, another speaker of a small and strange language (Saarikivi, 2021). His argument was that we are not only expressing our thoughts in a language but also thinking with it. One of Kaplinski's essays was titled 'What if Heidegger had been a Mordovian?' Indeed, unlike Mordovians, most of our brightest minds (Heidegger, Hegel, Kant, Sartre, Foucault, Schopenhauer, Gramsci, etc.) have all been able to think and write in their own language, since they have had enough readers in their national context. When they have become famous, their books have been translated into English and to other major languages. There are always things which are lost in translation, but those who are interested can always go to the original sources. This is not the case with small language communities, where particularly academics are more and more forced to read, write, and speak in English instead of their native language—for obvious reasons, since science is global and we all want to make an impact on the whole academic community, not to mention the rewards that universities are given for international publishing (which means publishing in English). In these cases, things are not lost in translation but from thinking itself.

Nevertheless, most of us have started our thinking with our native language, and obviously its concepts, categories, and structures stay with us. What if, for instance, it is not simply a coincidence that in the Finnish language there is no concept that would allow us to conflate living as a corporeal human being with living as a resident? The word *asua* does not only mean residing but it is also the root for *asettautua* and *asettua*, which both mean to stop moving, finding a place where one can stay. The latter can also metaphorically mean getting rid of one's radical ideas and restless life and start abiding by traditional norms. The noun *asema* (station) also refers to a place where movement is stopped, in the same way as the Latin origin of the English word means stationary and stay (statio, stare). The Finnish verb *elää*, on the other hand, does not refer to place at all. To the contrary: *eläväinen* means somebody who cannot stay still, and *elävä* is the opposite of *kuollut* (dead). When you are dead, you don't move any longer. Living is moving.

Actually, this is not the only instance where Finnish is different from the major European languages in terms of space and place. The word *planning* with its Latin origin in *planum* is repeated in most European languages (planering, pianificazione, planung, pianification, planificación, planeja-mento) and connects the activity to land, to the plane surface where build-ings are to be located. In Finnish, the corresponding word is *suunnittelu*, which means both planning and design. However, it does not refer to land at all, but to *suunta* (direction). Thus, literally it means deliberating or giving direction to movement or activities. If you stay in one place or in a (small) area, you don't need directions. If we go into details, the word *yhdyskuntasuunnittelu*, which is usually translated as urban and regional planning, comes from yhdyskunta (community). As we know, communities can move, whether they are ants, bees, or tribal communities. Tribal com-munities of hunters or nomads are rare nowadays, but this does not mean that movement would have stopped—nowadays they are mostly individuals and families who move.

Thus, we have difficulties in expressing the ontology of living-but-not-staying in English—something that is perfectly natural in my own native language. To prevent losing this essential distinction, we seem to need new concepts. In his famous novel from 1831, Nikolay Gogol coined the term 'dead souls' to refer to the people (serfs) who were already deceased but still existed in statistics, which made it possible to trade with them (Gogol, 2004). In our case, we are dealing with people who are not dead (actually very much alive as corporeal human beings) but who are not recognized by statistics for where they are. On the other hand, we have the statistical units (the registered persons) who do not have a corporeal existence but still have a location. When the corporeal man leaves for work in the morning, the statistical unit is left behind. He never moves away from his 'detailed small area' where he is registered. Only when death arrives, the corporeal and the state-man become one: the doctor declares the corporeal person dead (i.e. he becomes a corpse), and his death is registered. When living ends, so does movement. For lack of better words, let us call these two entities corporeal man and state-man (or woman).

The two ontological entities have very different characteristics. The corporeal human being takes one place at a time, spending there shorter or longer periods of time, confronted by other people who are physically nearby, touched, heard, smelled, or seen by him, himself being seen by them. People as corporeal human beings, as mind-bodies, are infinitely different from each other. All attempts to abstract them mean stripping them from some of their characteristics—and there are no self-evident criteria to determine which features are important enough to be saved. The statistical unit, in contrast, does not have a body or a mind. In addition to location, it has a sex, usually a man or a woman (although it cannot engage in sexual activities), age, and marital status. It has a history: between its birth and death, it has a linear sequence of moves from the place of birth to its subsequent residential locations (again, as statistical locations). As we have seen, the corporeal human being and the statistical unit are not co-existent with each other. Although some of the characteristics of the statistical unit can be seen as abstractions of the corporeal human being (such as age and sex), some others cannot (particularly location).

The interesting feature of these two entities is also their political role. Although the statistical unit, the state-man, does not have a corporeal existence, its political rights, such as the right to vote, are derived from its statistical location. It is also entitled to municipal services based on its location, even though he cannot use them. As a non-corporeal being without mind or will, it cannot benefit from these rights, but they have to be 'delivered' to the corporeal human being. The latter cannot demand, for instance, health care to where he actually lives, but he has to 'go home' to get them. Some other rights, such as the right to life or physical sovereignty are, in contrast, the rights of only the mind-body.

Although it may sound like hair-splitting, this ontological difference has important political consequences. By choosing to live (at least partly) in another location than the registered person, the corporeal human being effectively loses some of his political rights and, consequently, the governing authority, the national or local state, is free from its own obligations. In a way, we may say that the state is not planning its services, its land-use, or its infrastructure to the people (of flesh and blood) but to itself, or to the imagined community of registered residents whose welfare it is committed to—even though there cannot be welfare of the statistical units.

Suppose, then, that the man in our case notices that he would pay less of local taxes if he would 'live' in the city instead—the cities are usually economically stronger and can keep their local tax rate lower. He then informs the authorities that he has now 'moved' to his apartment in the city. Nothing happens in the physical world: he spends exactly the same amount of time in both locations, nothing is packed in boxes, no furniture is moved. Only the state-man moves from the countryside to the city. This is, however, what is noticed by the researcher who studies urbanization. He never sees the corporeal man—he doesn't have time, since he is doing quantitative studies, and meeting and interviewing thousands of people is not possible. But he does see the state-man who moved to the city—or not really, since it is invisible. In a way, statistics has created its own non-corporeal Cartesian ego: it is registered; therefore, it is.

Strange as it may seem, the *discursive turn* has now led us to the *corporeal turn*. Not only ontology but also the epistemology of urbanization is challenged. If we are interested in real people with flesh and blood and want to make *their* everyday life better through knowledge, we cannot use statistics. If we are using statistics, we are doing something else. But what?

This is a question that we need to return to in the next chapter on the epistemology of multi-locality. Before that, however, let us dwell for a while in this strange dualism of the corporeal and the state-man. The obvious critique against my argument is that our case is only a rare exception, since few people can afford to own or rent two apartments or are willing to travel weekly to a distant location. 'Multi-locality is a privilege of a small elite' as one of my critics wrote in his blog. Generalizability is, however, not the point here, and it is important to understand the role of the examples and counter-examples that I shall be using in this book. They are mostly real examples (stories of people of flesh and blood), although I sometimes change the parameters (as in the previous case with the state-man 'moving' to the city). I have gathered the stories from interviews, personal acquaintances, and public documents. In arguments, however, they are used as thought-experiments: a conceptual framework or a theory can be tested against case descriptions. If it cannot deal with them, there seems to be something wrong with it. In this sense, theories can be refuted or falsified not only by observations but also by counter-examples. In philosophy, these counter-examples are often deliberately unrealistic, since it is often in borderline cases that the inconsistency of our thinking is revealed. I have kept my cases more down-to-earth, but this seems to be enough, since I am not actually dealing with something extraordinary, not even a small elite.

What this first case demonstrates is that the methodologies based on statistics are essentially unreliable, since they are based on an implicit assumption that the corporeal human being and the statistical unit, the state-man, live in the same place, and that there is only one such place. Since this is not the case, we clearly cannot use the same methodology to justify the claim that there are only a few of such persons. That would simply be circular reasoning, a *petitio principii*. We have to admit that *we don't know* how many are there. In computer science, scholars warn us that if the data are not reliable, we cannot expect much of the results either, 'garbage in, garbage out'. For some reason, however, many social scientists and geographers don't seem to care.

Indirectly, on the other hand, we can have an idea of the supposed rarity of the cases. First of all, one does not have to be very rich to own or rent an apartment or a house in two different places. The price differences of urban versus rural housing makes this possible: instead of a large urban dwelling, one can have a smaller apartment in the city and a large one-family house in the countryside or in a smaller town. This is an opportunity for the middle classes, of course, not for the urban poor, but even those with lower wages may find a job only from another municipality, renting a small flat near their working place only for that purpose.

Additionally, we have a long tradition of second home ownership and use in many European countries. Spain is particularly a country with many second homes, making up to 14.6% of the housing market, exceeding 30% in some provinces and 90% in some municipalities. There was a boom in the 1970s and 1960s, based on the rising standard of living of the middle classes and opening up of the real estate market to foreign home-owners. It has also been the result of urbanization, since the homes left behind have often become second homes (Montoriol-Garriga, 2020).

In the Nordic countries, living in second homes has a long tradition, partly for the same reasons. They are called 'mökki' in Finland, 'stuga' in Sweden, and 'hytte' in Norway, which have originally meant modest holiday cabins used during the summer holiday and some weekends. Nowadays, many of them have the same facilities as urban houses, allowing year-around use, which has resulted in an increased rate of actual occupancy of the spaces. In Finland, for instance, the number of second homes has been rising steadily, as well as the number of nights spent in them. There are more than half a million second homes, with more than two million people using them on a regular basis, in a country of only 5.5 million people. In 63 municipalities, there are more second homes than permanent ones (Statistics Finland, 2020). Before the pandemic, the users were staying in their second homes for 79 nights yearly on an average. During the pandemic, this figure rose to 103, already 28% of the whole year. Out of those who could telework, 43% did it in their second home (Voutilainen et al., 2021). These are not small numbers; we are talking about the large middle classes, not only a small elite of multi-locals.

Considering these figures, it is interesting that only when the pandemic hit these European countries, the authorities suddenly 'noticed' that people are not actually living where they are supposed to live, and that they can react to unusual circumstances by changing their place. When the cities lost a major part of their attractions (restaurants, coffee shops, museums, movie theatres, libraries, music clubs, etc. were closed) and people were forced to work and study at home, those who had access to a second home made a rational choice and moved there. Instead of having a vacation, they could telework and study, and it was also easier to keep social distances in the countryside. Many of those who did not have access to a second home, started searching for one; The loans taken for second home purchases increased by 40% in Finland. The authorities realized that people moving from cities to smaller municipalities would burden the health-care systems of the small municipalities beyond their capacities. The answer to this dangerous scenario was simple: ordering people to go and stay 'home'. Whole regions were closed in, for instance, Italy, Spain, and Finland.

The reason for this panic was not that people would have behaved irrationally or irresponsibly—surely it *is* easier to keep social distances in less-urban regions, and staying in a small urban flat with two parents working online and children attending online school at the same time hardly represents an ideal solution, psychologically or socially. The problem was that the whole health-care system had been built on an assumed unilocality, not considering where people actually live but where they are registered. However, when the corporeal human beings moved to their second homes, the state-men stayed in the city, surrounded by services that they did not need. The viruses, on the other hand, are parasites that can only infect corporeal organisms like people, and people are the ones who need health care.

During several decades, the welfare state had been built, on the assumption that people are only living in one place, or almost all of them, or at least most of them, or at least most of the time. If they are not, they can always be ordered to 'go home'. The Spanish government declared a strict curfew, the Finnish government closed the most urbanized Uusimaa region, and the Prime Minister of India ordered his 1.3 bn population to go and stay home for at least three weeks, even though many of them had no home in the cities and had to hit the road. When the reality of people and the fiction of the governments don't match, it is so much the worse for reality.

Let us consider a second case description, a story of a Finnish couple whose multi-locality does not respect even national borders. They used to own a large and expensive waterfront apartment in Finland, but they noticed that most of the year it stood empty. The husband was already retired, and the wife was an entrepreneur who could work remotely, and thus they were rather independent of their geographical location. They already owned a second home in a holiday resort in Thailand, and they also liked cruising. Thus, they decided to sell the apartment in Finland and buy a smaller one instead. 'The main criterion was price: it had to be cheap', the wife said as I interviewed her. The remaining money they invested in another small apartment in Spain. Consequently, their time was spent in a triangle: like migratory birds, they moved to Spain or to Thailand when the weather turned bad and there was no sunshine in Finland. When they were not using either the Spanish or the Thai home, they could rent them out to compensate for the maintenance costs of the three apartments. Economically, this solution was quite feasible for a middle-class couple with grown-up children.

What do we make out of this triangle, theoretically? Do we have a first, a second, and a third home? Permanent or temporary? Work-based residence or tourism? None of the established categories seem to be suitable, and they also did not correspond to the perception of the couple, according to the wife whom I interviewed. At the time she was already retired like her husband, and thus they had even less geographical restrictions than before. Two of her grown-up children still lived in Finland, one in Spain and one in the USA, and thus the network of family relationships was also global. All of the three homes had been owned by them for years, and they were thus permanent, even though the Spanish and the Thai apartment could be rented out. They could work or spend their 'free' time in any of them, and thus none of the usual dichotomies based on work or tourism would make sense. The one in Finland was 'first' only in the sense that it was never rented and could thus be used as storage space. As corporeal human beings, they spent most of the time outside Finland, although they were registered in Finland.

Nevertheless, for the 'state-couple,' things appear quite differently. What does the law say about people who have several addresses, which they use regularly? This is how the lawmaker defines the domicile in their country, as late as in 2016, 'If a person has several places of residence or doesn't have any, his/her domicile is the one which he/she him/herself regards as his/her domicile, based on his/her family relationships, livelihood or corresponding circumstances, and to which he/she has the most fixed relationship based on the above-mentioned circumstances.' (11.3.1994/201, 2§, my translation[1]). The domicile is thus the city or the municipality where the person subjectively considers belonging to and to which she has the 'most fixed relationship'. This couple, however, does not have a fixed relationship to any of the three places, they are continuously on the move. Their grown-up children, on the other hand, are living in different countries, and even those still residing in Finland live in different cities. There is no obligation to work for retired people, and teleworking has been done in all of them. Their subjective experience, thus, cannot be based on these 'objective' circumstances, as the law requires.

For this couple, however, there actually *is* no such experience of a fixed domicile. When asked about a possible hierarchy between these three places, the wife had great difficulties in judging whether some of them would be primary or secondary. They are all homes, according to her, since they are owned by them, and they have been able to design and decorate them according to their own preferences. The Spanish and the Thai homes are kept somewhat more neutral, since they are rented out occasionally, but even there the paintings on the walls and furniture are important marks of ownership. They have had the home in Thailand longer than the one in Finland, and the children and grandchildren visit them there rather than in Finland. 'In our Finnish home we don't even have a sofa, only two beds.' It soon became clear that the question of the hierarchy of the three homes was artificial, based on a normative ideal of one permanent residence and possible second homes for 'vacation'.

Comparisons like this clearly reveal the problems in trying to integrate the corporeal existence of men and their statistical counterparts, the state-men.

It is typical of the former that they are mostly on the move, choosing places where they spend shorter or longer periods of time, with different meanings attached to them. Borders are mostly permeable to them: in the normal, pre-pandemic circumstances, they have easily moved over municipal, regional, and national borders, and the meanings attached to their many places are not mainly based on the territories where they belong to. The state-men, specified by statistics, politics, and planning, in contrast, are characterized by places: places of permanent residence or (longer) temporary residence and permanent workplaces. Thus, for them, it seems reasonable to define the territories that our policies and plans are targeted at.

In addition to the assumed size of cities (as the number of registered persons with more or less fixed places), another concept often used in our established discourses on urbanization is *growth*. We might do a similar analysis as we did with the concepts of *living*, starting with its meaning and ending with the corporeal existence that, as we have seen, tends to escape from our view. What does it mean to say that cities or urban regions are 'growing'? It is clear that this is a metaphor, taken from the world of nature and agriculture, and thus it 'naturalizes' something that is actually not organic; cities are not animals or plants. Unlike them, they do not grow by adding new residents on top or around the existing ones. This is what trees do: each year they develop a new layer of cells around the trunk, creating annual rings from which one can calculate their age when they have been felled. The 'growth' of the city is, in contrast, only a net sum from the number of registered people moving in and out of the city, as well as those who are born or die. The city is, in this sense, made up of constant mobility, even if we would only take into account the registered residents, the state-people. There is not a certain group of 'new' people entering the city and making it grow. The number of people entering the city in a specific year is many times larger than the net growth, but so is also the number of people leaving the city. On the other hand, the city as a physical space is not necessarily becoming any larger.

But why do we take it natural (sic) to call this 'growth', and not mobility, birth and death? Usually, we don't even notice that we are using a naturalistic metaphor. It is thus a 'dormant metaphor', analysed for instance by Perelman and Olbrechts-Tyteca. In their New Rhetoric, they have extensively studied the role of analogies and metaphors in persuasive communication (Perelman & Olbrechts-Tyteca, 1971). According to them, the dormant metaphors (ibid., p. 405) are concepts that have been so extensively used that they are worn out, becoming clichés or simple denotative words. Thus, we no longer notice that 'growth' is a naturalistic metaphor, since it has become so commonplace. According to Perelman and Olbrechts-Tyteca, the dormant metaphors need to be 'reawakened' to retain their persuasive force. Ideologically, however, they may be even more powerful when left dormant. Growth is a very positive concept in nature and agriculture, and using it in the context of economic development or urbanization carries with it this positive connotation. If we would use, for instance, cities 'gaining weight' or suffering from 'obesity', we would not only reveal that we are using metaphors, we would also imply the critical aspects of the phenomenon.

We can clearly see the artificiality of the concept of growth if we change the scale. An urban square has certain physical dimensions, but the number of people using it is different during different hours of the day. In the morning people enter, some passing by, some sitting in the bars or visiting the shops. Towards the night there are fewer and fewer people until it is almost empty. Why don't we say that the square is *growing* every morning until afternoon, after which it starts to decline? Functionally, the city is pretty much similar: every morning commuters from the surrounding municipalities enter the city to work there, leaving again in the evening. Tourists and other visitors sit on the terraces and restaurants and visit the shops. During the weekends, even many formal residents leave the city to their second homes. In both cases, the geographical dimensions of the city and the square may stay the same. Using the ontology of corporeal and state-ontology introduced above, we may describe what happens: the corporeal commuters (perhaps with their material cars) enter the city, while the state-men stay in the surrounding municipalities. The state-men of the city, on the other hand, stay in their housing neighbourhoods, while the corporeal people sit in the restaurants and visit the shops. The city is used, and it is used by moving around, both inside the city and over its municipal borders. Nevertheless, we choose to call the changes in the net number of state-men urban *growth*. For the square, no such statistics are indicating a 'net growth' of the square, and so the square does not grow, unless we demolish some of the buildings around it. Movement is real, growth is a fiction that we use selectively.

These observations suggest that, at the same time as urban and regional planning and governance are inherently territorial, the reality outside this rigid framework is increasingly escaping the boundaries and rules dictated by it. On the other hand, human spatial activities and locations are increasingly followed by global companies using modern technology, but this knowledge is mostly not available to the users themselves nor the traditional governing bodies—except the agencies dealing with state security. How can we understand this paradox, this incongruence between the imagined uni-local residents and workers, and the unknown and ungoverned practices that are emerging, forming their own spaces and logics—and at the same time being vulnerable to the 'predators' collecting data that they can use for their commercial purposes? The pandemic only highlighted the problematic of this paradox, as state authorities around the world have found it necessary to restrict the mobility and multi-locality that is an elemental feature of urbanity.

This is particularly interesting, since planning and governance are usually not directly addressing or problematizing this territorialism. People do not actually live *in* neighbourhoods, not socially nor physically, but planners are still *planning* neighbourhoods, bordered enclaves of housing and services around them, which are supposed to satisfy their residents' daily needs. We expect them to form *communities of neighbours* who live close by, each in their house or apartment. Actually, however, they mostly go somewhere else to work, to meet friends, to shop, to hobbies, to holiday trips, and to second homes. Even those who don't necessarily need to leave their house—such as housewives or retirees—usually don't just stay at home but head towards other locations that are important to them. The home may be, for most of us, a 'homebase' that we leave for work or journey and then come back. But why should we think that this one point of the universe, which we daily leave and come back to, is the *one* legitimate place where we are supposed to be located?

This corporeal turn, or 'yea-saying to life' as Nietzsche put it (Nietzsche, 1911, p. 72, et passim), is what I shall discuss in this book. It is challenging both theoretically and practically, since it touches our traditional way of conceptualizing the city and urbanization in terms of size, growth, density, and diversity, and it is also much more difficult to plan land-use and policies for the corporeal people constantly on the move, traversing local, regional, and national borders. This question is, obviously, much more complicated than it seems at first sight, but I shall try to outline preliminary theoretical openings to it. To do this, I need to travel through a variety of theoretical perspectives from several disciplines. I will refer to both classical and contemporary literature, but this is not a literature review, nor a book about books. My (at times provocative) references and interpretations of the literature are not meant to be representative of their authors or their oeuvre. Nevertheless, this is a book about concepts: my approach is an experimental journey to a possible understanding of spatial thinking, in which unilocality would no longer be the norm.

In the next chapters, I shall discuss the ontology and epistemology of multi-locality, but I shall not stay in abstract philosophical notions. Rather I shall discuss them in their political, social, and subjective contexts. The apparently 'self-evident' phenomenon of multi-locality—and particularly the fact that, because of being self-evident, it is seldom seriously addressed—opens an interesting challenge for research in several disciplines, as well as planning and related practices.

Notes

1. The clumsiness of this direct translation of the law (with he/she and his/her) is explained by the fact that in Finnish there are no gender differences, the word 'hän' refers to both sexes.

2 The epistemology of escape and predator epistemology

Knowing and failing to know multi-local spatiality

The corporeal understanding of human existence has a long history in Western thought, although it has not been as dominant as its opposite, the variety of doctrines based on concepts like 'ideal' or 'essence'. We can call these doctrines 'idealist', although not in the narrow sense of the word referring to the non-existence of the physical world. I shall not try to tell even a rudimentary story of this debate, nor analyse critically the different doctrines connected to it, since this is not a book of philosophy. Nevertheless, I shall draw from this tradition some of the main arguments that I find necessary in my attempt to understand the epistemological problems of multi-locality.

How can we know something about people who are in infinite ways different from each other and who are constantly on the move, without keeping any of their properties constant and without remaining in any of the several places along their way for long—to say nothing of one permanent place? This is the problem already recognized by Heraclitus: 'Heraclitus says, you know, that all things move and nothing remains still, and he likens the universe to the current of a river, saying that you cannot step twice into the same stream' (Plato, 1921, p. 402a). Since there is a constant change, our knowledge tends to become outdated the very moment that we try to formulate it, and it is already history when we manage to publish it. The scholars trying to follow the trends of urbanization try to use the most updated statistics, but it is often from the previous year or from the previous census. They may defend their results by saying that, since the population flows are slow enough, the figures are 'almost correct'. But as I demonstrated in the introduction, this is not actually the case: if the real (the corporeal) population of a municipality is more than doubled during the summer season or a weekend, the official population of the municipality is not 'almost the same' as the real population. As we saw in the case of the retired couple, this phenomenon is global: during the winter they head towards the sun, at the same time as the 'state-couple' remains in the dark and rainy Finland. And they are not the only ones: the proportion of the retired people without geographical restrictions is growing rapidly, particularly in Europe. The flow of people is in a way as fast as the flow of water in a stream, which we can clearly see by watching the flow of traffic on busy roads.

DOI: 10.4324/9781003124443-2

We may even take a step further and consider the real nomads who clearly go against the administrative assumption of a fixed location. Let us consider a third case story of a young man who works as a freelance journalist. He decides to travel through Europe to study the rising populist movements in various countries. He gives away his apartment, travelling by bike, bus, and plane, living in cheap hostels, and using his couch-surfing network. He writes articles on various subjects and lives with this revenue; journalism clearly does not require (or is not even possible by) sitting in an office. In order to have an address in his home country and receive the eventual physical letters (most of his mail being of course e-mails), he decides to 'move' to his parents' house, who can scan and send to him the possible invoices and other mail of importance. His corporeal existence, his locations, and mobility, are thus very different from the 'state-man' who 'moves back home', even though the corporeal man doesn't spend a single night there. He has clearly *escaped* from the view of the state authorities who have no way of following his changing locations. But he has also escaped from the researchers using statistics who might, for instance, be interested in knowing how many grown-up children still 'live' with their parents. Well, he would be one of them. State-knowledge is living in its own reality.

As we know, Plato tried to solve this problem by arguing that the constantly changing world is merely an imperfect reflection of ideas or forms that remain constant. This solution gave input to a whole history of idealistic and essentialist theories of reality, but it can also be said to be a precursor of contemporary natural sciences with their immutable laws of nature expressed in mathematical formulae, the famous 'book of nature' by Galilei (Galilei, 1623). The natural scientists have been successful in predicting the changes in the natural world with precision—unlike for instance the economists, who have not been able to predict the changes in the stock market or even the growth of the GDP. They do provide us with such predictions, but when these turn out to be false, they simply make new predictions. And as shown above, the social scientists clearly cannot follow the nomads or even people travelling to their second homes.

Nietzsche's famous critique against these idealist doctrines can be seen as a reversal of the arguments in the Platonic tradition. According to the latter, in order to give prevalence to the ideas, forms, or essences (which can be known) over the changing corporeal and material existence (which cannot), the latter had to be seen as mere appearances or unfinished and imperfect instantiations of perfect ideas. Consequently, as we start reflecting on these ideas or idealities, such as knowledge, rationality, right, good, beautiful, or moral, we have to keep our arguments separate from the immanence of the corporeal world. Thus, we don't deduce knowledge from the ways that people use this concept; epistemology is not derived from sociology of knowledge. Similarly, we don't base our view of rationality, aesthetic quality, virtue, or morality from the ways people tend to think or act, which things they consider beautiful or ugly, or how they differentiate right from wrong. Hume's law, the logical separation of facts from values, is still dominant in our thinking, even though there have been numerous attempts to bridge the gap.

Compared to these idealities, the actual human beings are naturally found deficient, and the next question is how to develop them towards the ideal human being, how to control and punish them to avoid crime and immorality, or how to educate them to think and act rationally. The tasks of bringing these imperfect and unfinished human beings, as well as their society and culture, closer to the ideal form are given to specific institutions: the school, the church, the army, the police, the prison, and other corrective institutions. It is no coincidence that the word 'formation' does not only refer to giving form but also educating and arranging moving troops, ships, or aircraft. The form is order, the world outside of it is chaos, barbarism, and bestiality.

The Nietzschean critique turns the burden of proof upside down. If we, in contrast, start from the actual human beings, the way they are, act, and think, we cannot start from a rational argument. The corporeal existence of human beings does not need arguments to be what it is. People are all different from each other, and they do not stay the same. They have urges, desires, and fears, which are directed towards their environment. They have knowledge of this environment (yes, corporeal knowledge, attained with their senses and thoughts with their brains and body). They build relationships with their fellow human beings, which can be friendly but also extremely violent. And they move around if they are not incarcerated.

How do we add the ideals in this picture, then, or do we need to? If we answer in the negative, we end up simply following what happens: how people think, act, and treat each other. If we don't want to retreat to this position of a neutral spectator, we need to find an argument for the superiority of the form against the multitude of actual beings, their features, and activities. Where is the legitimacy or the right of the institutions to educate, to control, to prevent, or even to destroy the individuals who do not con*form* to the pre-determined form? As soon as we ask this question, we immediately see that it is not so easy to provide such an argument. If the form is not automatically better than the existing reality, it has to be justified. Why is raising better than rising, or obeying better than deciding? Is it possible to educate without first defining the ideal personality (form) towards which education is directed and against which its success is measured? If not, where does this form come from, and how much can we expect the students to conform to it?

What does this mean, then, in our case? The state-man carries many of the characteristics of the Platonian form: it is invisible, and although it has a location and can move from one address and city to another, it is abstract, consisting of a number of registered features. Collectively, these features make up aggregate numbers: how many people are there in a given area, how many of them are women, how many have a college education, etc. But since this is not real (i.e. the real people mostly live their life somewhere else, having features that are not at all abstract), what kind of forms are they? Are they ideals? Could we say that living in a certain address and staying there is good or morally better than moving around? This seems questionable, but on the other hand the pandemic has again shown the force of the state: it has been possible for the state to order people to 'go home' and 'stay at home', while they have been forbidden to move to their second homes or use many of the services in the city.

One of the counter-arguments that I have met as I have discussed these different types of multi-locality is that there is nothing new, that all of this is already known: people having second homes, working in another city, owning an apartment in Spain, or travelling through Europe without any permanent address. And my critics have been quite right: there is nothing new, we all know these things. The problem is, however, that even though we know it, our state-epistemology, or state or Royal science (science d'Etat) as Deleuze and Guattari call it in their 1980 book Mille Plateaux (Deleuze & Quattari, 2019, pp. 422–423), does not even try to handle this phenomenon 'which we all know'. Why is this? Clearly this is not a question of adding more knowledge or repeating our existing knowledge of the phenomenon of multi-locality. We have to study it within its context, and this context is the state, from which the word 'statistics' originates.

Here we are moving on dangerous ground. The state and the academia have traditionally had their distinct idealities. The state is a power-generating and power-using machinery; its decisions are based on force derived from the monopoly of violence (not force of the best argument, as Habermas would have it). We can consider its legitimacy or the political system that ensures it, and this is the ideal usually connected to it. Academia, on the other hand, defends its position as an independent institution with academic freedom to do research and teach. Mixing these two idealities is thought to be detrimental to both: direct political influence only creates poor science, and poor science is not a very useful tool in policy making. The politicization of research in the former Soviet Union is often given as a warning example of how science deteriorates if it needs to pretend that its results always support the existing regime.

The problems of this dichotomy are, however, easy to see. If the state is the main funding source of academic research and teaching, how can it fail to influence the way that research is done, making it 'politically correct'? How can critical analysis of the state—or even the university itself as a social institution—be possible? It is clear that the state does not have to dictate research. Researchers and the university institutions can do it by themselves, either deliberately or without noticing, just by following the 'research-strategies' and the funding mechanisms adopted by the state. The universities are dependent on them.

Statistics and the disciplines (sic) using them obediently are a good case of this grey area of state-research or Royal Science. Historically, the word comes from the eighteenth century as *Statistik* but, as Foucault writes, already in the seventeenth century it was understood that the knowledge necessary for the sovereign was not only the legal basis of the state but the strength and qualities of the population (Foucault, 2004). This observation led to the famous concept of biopolitics, still relevant in understanding contemporary urban governance and planning. What is interesting, in addition, is that Foucault—referring to Palazzo (1606)—connected statistics not only to the state but also to *status* (being in a state of immobility, static) and being in a good order (en état). This heritage questions the ideal image of statistics and social sciences derived from it as neutral and independent. It also highlights the connection of power and staying in one place; only immobile people can be governed.

Having his background in critical theory, Jürgen Habermas took the challenge of questioning this ideal image of an independent and neutral knowledge in his book *Knowledge and Human Interests* from 1968 (Habermas, 1981). Criticizing Husserl, he stated that the classical tradition of theory and the subsequent development of the sciences explain our contemporary difficulties in dealing with the (self-identified) positive sciences and normative social ideals:

> Theory in the sense of the classical tradition only had an impact on life because it was thought to have discovered in the cosmic order an ideal world structure, including the prototype for the order of the human world.
>
> (ibid., p. 306)

As social sciences developed into positive sciences and left cosmology behind, they were also left on their own in terms of the normative content: ideal societies or proper human conduct could no longer be read from the stars or—as in the middle ages—from scriptures. The original connection between the state and its sciences—les sciences de l'état—did not disappear, however, in spite of the objectivist illusion. What is considered relevant knowledge is still connected to the political interests of the state, even to the extent that research is expected to provide 'policy advice' and 'social impact'. The 'impossibility' of critical theory is the logical corollary of this hidden interdependence.

From the point of view of this tradition, it is not self-evident that the lack of knowledge of the corporeal spatial existence of people—or even the lack of an interest in providing such knowledge—is a problem as such. If it would be so that statistics and social sciences based on them are essentially providing knowledge for the governing authorities, demanding more and more precise knowledge would implicitly take a stand for such governance. State-science has the interest of strategic control, not emancipation, something that Habermas would suggest as a more critical interest for the social sciences.

What could, then, be the theoretical perspectives allowing us to explain and understand this complex phenomenon of multi-locality that seems to defy traditional statistical methodologies? Clearly the idealities of state-men is not the only ontological perspective, and we have had traditions that allow approaching the corporeal and material reality more directly. In his paper on residential multi-locality, Peter Weichhart (2015) discusses three major strands of thought which are, according to him, incommensurable but could provide 'epistemological complementarity on a meta-level' (ibid., p. 389). The first of these is the tradition that we have discussed above, something that he also finds problematic:

> If we wish to remain on a merely descriptive level and explore the quantitative extent and spatial distribution of the phenomenon, we need to rely on the data of demographic statistics [...] In doing so, we have no other choice but to adopt the conceptual presuppositions of official statistics, which includes a reductionist concept of households (predominantly the household-dwelling concept), particular concept of 'residence', as well as the technical specifications and definitions of the respective national registration laws.
>
> (ibid., p. 380)

The two other options that he discusses are more promising, since they refer directly to corporeality: Hägerstrands's theory of time geography, originally from the 1970s, and the growing interest in things and materiality in social sciences, the so-called 'material turn'. We need to discuss them in more detail, particularly as they have established themselves in geography, social sciences, and planning theory.

In its core idea, Hägerstrand's theory is rather simple and intuitive: the human beings as corporeal bodies are geographically located, and their potential mobility is restricted by certain constraints. The movement or mobility of bodies in space, according to Hägerstand, can be biological, such as the ability and slow pace of walking, technological, such as the (un) availability of means of transport, or authoritative, such as the obligation to appear at the workplace at a certain time. Since we can only walk so far, are dependent on the availability of a private car or public transport, and usually need to sleep somewhere and go to work or school on time, our daily life 'has to exist spatially on an island' (Hägerstrand, 1970, pp. 12–13).

> *People need to have some kind of home base*, if only temporary, at which they can rest at regular intervals, keep personal belongings and be reached for receiving messages. And once a place of this sort has been introduced, one can no longer avoid considering more closely how time mixes with space in a non-divisible time-space. Assume that each person needs a regular minimum number of hours a day for sleep and for attending to business at his home base. *When he moves away from it, there exists a definite boundary line beyond which he cannot go if he has to return before a deadline.*
>
> (ibid.)

However, Hägerstrand did not yet include the existing and emerging multi-locality in his conceptual framework. He saw that the availability of important spatial resources, such as dwellings, employment, and education, were 'outside the immediate control by the average citizen. He can sometimes migrate of course to some other settings. But when he is there, he will again find himself hooked up in the pre-existing arrangement which largely has to be taken as it is' (Hägerstrand, 1977, p. 61).

Nonetheless, Weichhart (2015) argues that the concept of capability constraint can be straightforwardly applied in explaining residential multi-locality: if an individual intends or has to perform regular activities at a place which is located outside the definite boundaries defined by his current home base, 'he/she needs to create and utilise a second home base at this other place' (Weichhart, 2015). But if a second 'home base' can be created (and why not a third, or a fourth...?), the boundaries are clearly not definite, and our individual is not living 'hooked' in an island, under the 'tyranny of time and space' (Weichhart, 2015, referring to Haggett, 1979 and Kramer, 2012). Hägerstrand admits that the home base can be temporary, but he tacitly seems to assume that there is a linear sequence of home bases, just like in the official statistics. Nevertheless, if the definition of a home base is that one sleeps and keeps one's belongings there, then a hotel room can equally well be called a home base, extending the meaning of this metaphor far from its origins in games or military operations. How should we, for instance, describe the time-space of a nomad who is continually changing the place where he sleeps and keeps his (few) belongings? Receiving messages, mentioned by Hägerstrand, is no longer dependent on landlines or postal addresses.

There seem to be two main questions that we need to consider if we wish to apply Hägerstrand's theory to multi-locality. We may ask, first of all, if starting with the negative word *constraint* is most useful in characterizing the space-time of people who are on the move and stay in several places. Implicitly, it is like starting from an infinite imaginary universe that the individual has power over before he is imprisoned in his 'Rykers Island'. If we, in contrast, approach the universe from the point of view of individual mind-bodies, their potential movements in the space around them can more adequately be described as extensions—i.e., we would move from negative to positive freedom. Physical practicing may allow us to walk faster and longer journeys, and taking different technologies to use extends the space of potential places even further. Not even sky is the limit.

Second, we naturally have to take into account that Hägerstrand's theory was developed in the 1970s before the internet, wi-fi, and mobile phones. These technologies have radically changed the time geography that—according to Hägerstrand—was constrained by the slowness of human corporeal mobility, as well as the only available fast technology, the telephone. These made him to introduce the 'coupling constraints', the difficulties of people to get into contact with each other. In addition to the necessary travelling to reach other people, even the telephone had its limitations:

> Even if members of a population do nothing else than engage in sending messages of different length by telecommunication media (so that transportation for all practical purposes is instantaneous) the indivisibility of the human being is a severe constraint on what can happen. As soon as a communicating group has come into being, the duration of its activity inevitably creates waiting times among those who want to come into contact with one or more members of the group. The conflicts that arise will become a more and more obvious difficulty as we move towards a society in which the handling of information develops into the main activity, whether for economic, educational, political, personal service or recreational purposes.
>
> (Hägerstrand, 1977, p. 64)

Those of us who still remember the frustration of trying to reach somebody by phone or 'waiting by the phone' connected to a landline (when this 'telecommunication medium' was still the only available means of instant communication over long distances) can understand Hägerstrand's argument, but he was not much of a futurologist: economic, educational, political, personal service, and recreational purposes have today a very different toolbox: e-mails and e-mail lists, teleconferencing, social media, online services, internet games, etc. allowing personal, group-, or public interaction. You can couple with friends or thousands of people, and if some of them start annoying you, you may also de-couple yourself.

When the geographical distance is brought to the picture, Hägerstrand sees there an added complexity that cannot be avoided:

> It is first of all unavoidable that facilities where sub-operations of the programme [pre-planned time-table to perform an operation] have to take place are separated by distances. This adds time for movement. How much depends on the programme. As a rule, the more of division of labour and specialization of function one has foreseen the more bits of transportation will have to be provided. It is further unavoidable that facilities will have certain capacity limitations. These produce waiting-times in queues. It is unavoidable that people, when moving from location to location in the area, become involved in unforeseen events depending upon how things and activities happen to get packed together in the limited space. In short, the ideal space-free time-table does not work.
>
> (ibid., p. 64)

Unlike faster trains and automobiles, however, ICT has created a time-space compression that allows being virtually present while being physically absent.

This also means that the essential part of the tyranny of space and time, the 'definite boundary line beyond which he cannot go if he has to return before a deadline' has disappeared—for those who have the potential and do not need to 'return before a deadline'. This also means that we cannot restrict our attention to the body only as a biological entity. We are not equal in our health, our access to cars, planes, or even buses or, finally, in our ability to telework. Concentrating on positive rather than negative freedom allows us to include this economic and social inequality in our theory of multi-locality. In that sense, the metaphors of island and tyranny are to the point: weaker economic situation or lower employment status also means a more constrained space-time. However, changing our conceptual framework from negative constraint (what you cannot do) to positive freedom (what you can do) may be more fruitful for an analysis of multi-locality.

Nevertheless, Hägerstrand's conceptual framework includes an important element that I shall discuss in the next chapter. Although his ontology was corporeal, in the sense that he considered the constraints of the human body and its movements, his space-time prisms also referred to modalities: what the individual can do (but does not necessarily do) and what he is supposed to do (under the authority of the different domains, such as his workplace). When analysing the (by then) normal workday, he assumed that the worker needed to be at the workplace for a certain number of hours (which closed his options), and that the 'remaining prism breaks up into three portions, one in the morning before work, one at the lunch hour, and one in the evening after work' (Hägerstrand, 1970). Thus, the domain of the workplace was a controlling mechanism, outside of which the individual had some freedom to choose.

However, it is easy to see how difficult—or perhaps even useless—it is to apply this original framework to the multi-local work using ICT. Consider a worker who is assigned with a task (through e-mail), and who has access to the information that she needs in the company database. In addition to the task, she is naturally given a deadline, and she needs to return the work within the time frame to her supervisor. Outside this, she is totally free to organize her work-time and her whereabouts. She will surely have a 'path', but it can only be detected afterwards. Along the way she may have several places of residence ('homebases', if you like), but these are all chosen by her. Would it make much sense to characterize her work in the project as a giant prism, which is even open-ended? Since there are much less constraints, describing her situation from the positive point of view (as possibilities, or potentialities) would seem more natural.

The third perspective that Weichhart (2015) discusses can generally be called the 'material turn'. It is an extension of the corporeal turn: bodies are naturally material things, but they also live among a multitude of non-human animals and inanimate things. These have to be taken into account if we wish to describe and understand human agency in the material world. One of the classics opening this branch of research was Bruno Latour's and Steve Woolgar's book *Laboratory Life: The Construction of Scientific Facts* from 1979 (Latour & Woolgar, 1986). It was a strange and provocative book, since it was based on a fieldwork that Latour carried out in Roger Guillemin's scientific laboratory at the Salk Institute—without being a scientist. The result was not a scientific report but a description of a scientific practice, how research was made in that specific laboratory. Instead of studying the intellectual work of scientists, he approached them like an anthropologist studying a primitive tribe: observing their communication, their tools, their social roles, and their symbol systems. The attempt was to integrate the intellectual and social dimensions of science (hence the title 'laboratory *life*'), even to the extent that *facts* or even *logic* were considered to be constructed through this social practice.

Even though most scientists and philosophers of science would reject such a sociological or anthropological reading of scientific facts, the results of Latour's and Guillemin's work and the later Actor Network Theory (Law & Hassard, 1999) opened an interesting perspective to human agency among non-humans and things. Non-human animals and things can also be said to have agency; even if they are not intentional or conscious, they are still doing things, and this agency is also essential in understanding human agency. This may sound unintuitive but, on the other hand, our language does allow such agency ('The storm prevented us from going to the sea', 'The falling tree hit me', 'The computer performed its task very slowly'). What is important in this perspective is an inherent 'flat ontology' that resists binary and vertical categorizations (e.g. globalization affecting localities, power restraining human agency) and explaining things through their relationality, affecting each other. If we want to explain how things causally happen (even how new scientific knowledge comes into being), we need to consider what kind of things scientists actually (materially) confront with. They are not 'theories', 'observations', or 'existing knowledge' but rather textbooks, articles, oral presentations by other scientists, computer printouts, etc. In addition to their colleagues, these are agents—or actants—with which they need to work, as well as the more technical equipment such as calendars, telephones, test tubes, etc. The more abstract entities exist, of course, but they cannot materially participate in what is happening.

Considering the theories discussed above, we could now follow our previous strategy and dive into the corporeal existence and spatiality of human beings, in order to study how their knowledge is formed through individual knowledge-formation. This will also allow us to critically examine some of the wide-spread theories of space which, in addition to helping our understanding of multi-locality, can also be seen as obstacles.

Let us consider a perfectly normal workday of a woman working remotely with her computer. After sitting for several hours by her desk she decides to stretch her legs and take a walk. She chooses a nice path through a park, passing by places that she knows from previous walks. She meets some other pedestrians, listens to birds, and stops at the waterfront to watch the sea. After an hour, she returns to her work.

What is actually happening here, based on this description? First of all, it is clear that we are not talking about the state-woman: we did not mention where she is registered, in the municipality where she is working, or somewhere else. She is a corporeal human being, since she is sitting and walking. We equally do not know whether her desk is at her apartment, at her summer cottage, at a hotel, or even in a campervan. Wherever it is, it is clearly a workplace, a place where she works. It is a place where she has some kind of sovereignty (owning, renting or in some other way appropriating it). It has some qualities and meanings, since she has chosen to work in it. Nevertheless, since no authority is constraining her mobility (unlike in the Hägerstrandian domain), she can easily take a walk on the waterfront. This mobility is clearly in an important relationship to the place where she works: the place is something that she departs from and returns to. Thus, the concept of place implies other places and moving to them—or not being able to move to them. Even a prison cell refers to places outside the prison, places one cannot go to. The place thus conceptually refers to the space around it. A corporeal existence in one place is surrounded by innumerable places which are potential locations.

What is also interesting in this case is that both the place and the mobility are meaningful to the worker. Just like she has chosen the workplace for certain qualities, she also chose the path through the park and to the waterfront, obviously for some other qualities (fresh air, greenery, birds, scenery, etc.). One can also say that it is part of the qualities of the place that one has access to other places of different qualities. If she uses a campervan as her mobile office, she can also change the scenery and the places of interest around the whole office. She is not constrained in the Hägerstrandian sense, since there is no place where she would need to return to at a certain time. She needs to sleep, but she can do it in several places.

This observation is, however, in contrast with some of the most persistent traditions in conceptualizing places and spaces. We can hear, for instance, that places are more meaningful, that we have attached emotional meanings to them. We can also hear that places are more concrete, more down-to-earth than space, which is abstract. This is how Yi-Fu Tuan, for instance, describes this dichotomy in his book *Space and Place* from 1977:

> In experience, the meaning of space often merges with that of place. "Space" is more abstract than "place". What begins as undifferentiated space becomes place as we get to know it better and endow it with value [...] From the security and stability of place we are aware of the openness, freedom, and threat of space, and vice versa. Furthermore, if we think of space as that which allows movement, then place is pause; each pause in movement makes it possible for location to be transformed into place.
>
> (Tuan, 2011, p. 6)

But if we try to apply this dichotomy to our case of the teleworker, or many others for that matter, these concepts don't seem to fit into the picture. How could we say that the space (the path, or the set of potential paths) would be more abstract than the place where she works? Both can of course be *abstracted* into, for instance, the Cartesian grid and one of its points as vectors. But as things are in the corporeal world (which is never abstract, made of the Platonic forms), both the workplace and the recreational path are meaningful, although they have different meanings. She can never enter an 'undifferentiated' space: even when she visits a place for the first time or sets out to a journey through an unknown territory, she must already have a mental structure for it through narratives, experiences told by others, or by studying a map—otherwise she would never get there.

Similarly, the meanings that Tuan attaches to places and spaces are hardly generalizable. Places are not necessarily stable or secure or spaces free or threatening. Women who live with violent husbands without having the strength to leave are experiencing constant threat at home, as are workers who are subject to daily mobbing by their co-workers or superiors. For them the existence of space in the sense of other places and mobility is indeed a matter of freedom but also security, freedom from a place that they want to avoid or—paradoxically—are unable to avoid at the same time. On the other hand, places such as homes are often redecorated—and thus are not stable—even more often than their surroundings, such as the streets, parks or the waterfront.

Considering the relationship between space and time, one can also ask whether places are inherently connected with pauses. In our case, the woman may pass by several places known by her (a big tree, a pond, a flowerbed, a bench by the sea) without necessarily pausing in any of them. This is confirmed by our language: if somebody answers her mobile phone (without pausing), she can clearly say 'I am at the Senate Square, I will meet you at the restaurant in five minutes'. The square has both a historical depth and a personal relationship to her, but she doesn't need to *pause* in order to *be* at the place.

One may wonder where Tuan's dichotomy—which has lived on—is originally from. He gives no argument or reference, but there is something familiar in it: the moral superiority of place over mobility discussed earlier. Place naturally makes it easier to control us, and in order to use power over us, we need to be stopped. If the authorities know where we are, they can always come and get us, and ultimately stop our movement for good. Similarly, if the object of knowledge can only be something immobile and constant—not something moving and changing constantly—it is natural that the epistemology of the state-sciences is concentrating on places, even to the extent of confusing the places that corporeal people occupy and the places of their formal, registered existence. Providing services to these—and only these—locations, is a soft way of making sure that people don't go too far or stay there for too long, and that they can always be ordered to go 'back home'.

Going back to our teleworker, it is clear that she knows herself where she is, and she also knows her environment, partly through experience, partly through representations, such as maps. Experience is gathered as she learns more about the opportunities open to her, as well as the risks to be avoided. 'Knowledge that' is mingled with 'knowledge how', learning about the environment is also knowing how to deal with it. And what is important: this is not only positive (descriptive) knowledge but also normative. In order to be able to choose a possible path, she needs to know at least rudimentarily the legal framework, which is different in different countries. For instance, the right to pass through a private property is guaranteed by so-called 'everyman's right' in Finland, Norway, and Sweden, with the exception of private courtyards and cultivated fields in summer. In England and Wales, on the other hand, this right to roam applies only to some categories of uncultivated land. Public roads and parks naturally provide open access.

But in addition to knowing her legal rights, she also gradually learns the unwritten rules of the community where she resides or works. One must know, for instance, how long distances one should keep when passing by strangers. Unlike argued by Gehl (2010), there are cultural differences with respect to this social distance (Sorokowska et al., 2017). The pandemic, of course, brought with it a new meaning for social distance, indicating the physical distance between human bodies to prevent infection. Different localities also have unwritten rules for social behaviour: while it would be rude to greet or even stare at strangers in an urban context, the opposite may be the case in a rural location. For permanent settlers these rules are learned through experience, but for mobile dwellers and workers the situation is more challenging. It is important to understand, for both of them, that these rules are local and thus contextual: one abides by them to avoid social conflict. They are thus relative but not subjective: much of the debates in moral philosophy on whether moral truths are objectively true or subjectively held seem to be out of place in the contextual landscape, where one meets fellow citizens and wants to maintain good relationships to them.

The famous Simmelian metropolitan mentality, with its rational social relationships and blasé attitude, should thus be understood as contextual adaptation to the local requirements of the metropolis. Multi-local people need to be flexible: in the urban environment the same person may adopt the only social attitude that is relevant, passing strangers or even neighbours without a glance, whereas in the context of her second home she may talk to the shopkeeper or restaurant owner and ask help from her neighbour. The fewer people there are, the more important it is to maintain good relationships with them.

If this contextual epistemology is now compared to the official epistemology of the state-sciences, the difference is substantial. As mentioned, the latter is totally lost when it comes to the location of our teleworker:

where she sleeps, works, cooks, watches the television, and with whom. It can only analyze the environment around the official address, given by statistics. Even most of the characteristics of this environment are taken from statistics: the number of jobs in the vicinity, the available services, or the amount of green space around the place in which she is supposed to 'stay'. Just like people don't live only in one location, they don't stay there.

The ignorance of the corporeal and material reality also extends to the normative context: if and when state-science does not know where the corporeal human being is, it cannot know what kind of social environment is relevant to her, and when. This is particularly problematic in land-use planning, one of the practices that are dependent on official statistics. In addition to the state-men already living (sic!) in the area that is being planned, planners calculate how many people will move there when it is finished. The challenge is then to imagine what kind of people these are, what do they need, and what kind of social community will develop there. Since they are supposed to stay (sic!) in their houses or apartments, the services need to be provided around these places. But what are these 'once and future citizens' to whom planning is providing them?

In 2019, the city of Helsinki decided to build a new nursery for 150 children in the Kumpula neighbourhood. It had been planned already in 1996, but the site with its beautiful cliffs had remained empty until then, and the residents had been using it for recreation. When the decision of the planning authorities became public, a strong resistance from the residents emerged. They did not oppose the nursery itself (services like this were needed), but they did not understand why it had to be placed so that the whole cliff would be blown up. This was particularly strange, as there was another site next to it, where a primary school had been located but demolished. It was also owned by the city, but it was not planned for a nursery. During the conflict, the planning authorities gave no justification for the planned location, but they only argued that changing the plan and the design of the building would take too much time. That sounds strange after 25 years, but what happened was that the city was trying to find places where the detailed plan was already legally in force. They also noted that when the plan was originally made, in 1996, the citizens had already been heard. In addition to being approved by the city council back then, it was already 'interacted' (vuorovaikutettu), as they said. The citizens' opposition was of no avail, and the cliffs were blown up in January 2021.

In cases like this, the interesting question is what is meant by 'citizens' or 'residents'. These terms are often used without specification, even though it is well known that the group of people referred to does not stay the same. Even if we would concentrate only on the state-people (i.e. those who have registered this neighbourhood as their primary place of residence), approximately one fifth of these residents move each year. Thus, it is theoretically possible that the group of people who interacted with the planners in 1996 had been totally replaced by a new group in 1996.

If there had been families with small children, these children were already in university or work-life in 2021. The new residents needed day-care too (and did not oppose the nursery), but they were unable to influence its location. For the future residents, on the other hand, the new nursery is an asset that will influence their willingness to buy or rent an apartment in the neighbourhood, and they will have no recollection of the cliffs that it replaced.

The ontology of residents in a planned neighbourhood is thus rather complicated. The children who are nursed in the new building will of course be corporeal, as well as the people who had used the place for recreation. The children also have to be taken to the nursery and fetched from there, corporeally, usually by their parents. The assumption of planners and decision makers that the parents would be coming from their apartments in the neighbourhood is, however, ungrounded. Children are usually taken to nurseries when their parents return to work after their maternity leave. The probability to find a suitable workplace close to one's apartment is low, unless one is able to work from home. Consequently, having your children in a nursery closer to the workplace, rather than the home address, would make more sense. But, as we have seen, even corporeal services such as nursing or health care do not follow corporeal people. In Finland, all children have a subjective right to day-care, but only within the confines of their official neighbourhood. Thus, there is no need for the planners and decision makers to know the real locations and spatial needs of the citizens of flesh and blood.

Since there is clearly a difference between the experiential knowledge of the mind-bodies and the state-knowledge provided by traditional social sciences using statistics, the former in a way escapes from it, leaving the state in the dark. We can thus call it the *epistemology of escape*. But how far can an individual really escape from the state apparatus? The families with small children who have to take them to a nursery and fetch them on time, if they cannot afford to hire a private nurse to their home, are dependent on the distance to the nursery. School children also need to go to school on time, and this cannot be too far from their home. Thus, the welfare state has in a way taken the role of the workplace of Hägerstrand's reflection: if one is dependent on the municipal services, one needs to organize one's life around the fixed locations where time and space meet each other.

On the other hand, families with small children are only a part of the total number of households, and their share has dropped dramatically in developed countries, along with the declining fertility rates. In Helsinki, where our case was from, only 22% of the households were families with children in 2019, and only 15% were traditional nuclear families. The large majority of households have no such restrictions, and the time-geography of corporeal people is not confined within the perimeters of the neighbourhood. Planning has rightly been criticized for planning mainly the nuclear families in mind, although they have lost their dominant status a long time ago.

One may ask, then, whether this is simply a question of a lack of knowledge, something that could be solved by a new state-epistemology. This should be able to capture the real time-geography of people, where they stay and for how long, in order to provide the services that they need, wherever they are. On the other hand, escape is also a positive concept, as the opposite to confinement by the state apparatus. Are we really aiming at a *capture* of multi-local people, by reducing the freedom generated by the very existence of the gap between the corporeal experience and state epistemology? By the same token, our own scholarly efforts would become part of the state-sciences serving the state apparatus. Critical intentions would fade away, along with the freedom made possible by the escape.

Nevertheless, it is clear that the situation described above has already changed. The epistemology of escape is being taken over by what could be called *predator epistemology*. Citizens have voluntarily given access to their geographical information, detailed information on where they are and for how long. In return, they get private services, such as interactive maps, sports tracking and other targeted information that they might need or want. In this way, they also make themselves targets for commercials; they are indeed *captured* by private IT companies, and their data are also sold to other companies. As for instance Edward Snowden's revelations have shown, even in democratic countries this information is also used for state control, but for totalitarian regimes the new technology has no limits. If our movements, the places where we spend time, the people we meet, along with our movements in the virtual spaces of the internet, are detected and stored, state control is almost total—indeed totalitarian.

The interesting thing is, however, that the administrative state apparatuses of democratic countries have not been interested in developing epistemologies that would better correspond to the actual bodily movements of their citizens, even though technologies for this purpose would be available. This is clearly not only an ethical issue—democratic governance being committed to the values and rights of free mobility and settlement—since even the existing practice of statistics is based on the citizens' legal obligation to inform their addresses, either permanent or temporary. Even staying at a hotel is not 'hidden', but the guests have to be identified and, for justified reasons, their movements can be followed.

One may ask, thus, how state epistemology is structured around individuals, and on what interests it is based. One possibility to address this seeming paradox is to use two of Michel Foucault's observations of the changes in local and state governance: targeting the governing interest to populations instead of only individual bodies and acts, and biopolitics, the interest in the biological features of the population (Foucault, 1997).

The welfare state and planning as an elemental part of it can naturally be seen in this framework. It has been particularly interested in health care, such as child mortality rates, occupational health, environmental health and disease control (Foucault, 1997, pp. 69–71). These are all relevant to ensure that the nation has a large and strong enough population for the necessary production of goods and services. On the other hand, this population has to be kept in work-life so long that the costs of the welfare state can be covered. This is a persistent paradox of the welfare state, since many of the services and benefits (such as early retirement age and benefits, maternity leave and benefits, sick leave, unemployment benefits, etc.) at the same time create incentives to avoid work (if we use the language of the *homo economicus*), or at least make it possible if other preoccupations are preferable. To prevent this, measures to control the features of the corporeal human being are needed, for instance by making sure that those on sick leave and those who want to have an early retirement for health reasons are really sick and not just pretending. The interest of the state is, however, targeted at the whole population, not the individual mind-bodies.

> [T]he management of this population required, among other things, a health policy capable of diminishing infant mortality, preventing epidemics, and bringing down the rates of endemic diseases, of intervening in living conditions in order to alter them and impose standards on them (whether this involved nutrition, housing, or urban planning), and of ensuring adequate medical facilities and services.
>
> (ibid., p. 71)

In the same way, biopolitics is what dominates the way that abstract concepts are used in planning and urban policies. Here we can also refer to the earlier Foucault and his concept of 'discourse formation' referring to the 'rarity' of the concepts and arguments that serious speakers (in this case planners and policymakers) can use (Foucault, 1985b). According to Foucault, these are based on rules that need to be followed but are not consciously adopted. As the term 'archaeology of knowledge' indicates, these rules need to be excavated out. Considering planning and urban policy, the dominant typologies of people as the objects or 'clients' of planning (age, ability/disability, family, sex) and the typologies of the functions and impacts of planning (health, recreation, childcare, elderly care) are much the same as the features that we can detect from statistics, i.e. properties of the state-people. Situations such as the pandemic when health of the population is endangered, however, raise the location and mobility of people to the forefront. But even if health dangers and impacts are relevant only to the body-mind, the measures adopted are targeted at the whole population, not only at those who are infected or ill. Since anybody can be spreading the virus without knowing it, everybody is treated as a potential carrier of the disease, and their movements and behaviour are legitimately restricted.

3 Modalities of power
What are the many places for their users, and who can use them?

'I could have gone to the movies last night, but instead I stayed at home'.

This simple sentence—easily understood by everyone—represents a type of logic that has kept philosophers busy for centuries, particularly as they have tried to develop formal languages and semantics for such notions as possibility, potentiality, knowledge, belief, perception, memory, i.e. modal notions. This is not our concern here, but I try to demonstrate why we need to visit also this literature. First, as we need to have an understanding of the spaces that our multi-locals are operating in, modalities need to be addressed, and we also cannot understand urbanity without them. Second, this logic questions the corporeality that we have been defending so far.

If you consider this sentence, it has two elements: what happened and what could have happened. We can also clearly see that it is a sentence that can only be used by somebody who lives in (or is visiting) the city. Movie theatres are the first private services to disappear when the municipalities or towns start to shrink, if there ever were such amenities. Going to see a movie out of an impulse is not something that you do if you live in the countryside (or more accurately, *when* you live in the countryside). If you are multi-local, then it is quite natural to use these services available when you are in the city.

The reason why this has perplexed philosophers is easy to see. What happened is rather easy to understand; it is a description of the location of the corporeal human being during the night referred to. It would have been possible to observe what happened, either by visiting him or following the location data of his mobile phone. If this were part of a police interrogation, they would be interested in whether someone can confirm the story (for instance, if it would be an alibi).

But what about going to the movies? Since it did not happen, it could not have been observed with any method. It is not a fact in a sense of material happening. It is something that our corporeal human being did not do. However, saying that 'I could have gone to the movies' is not the same as saying that 'I did not go to the movies'. We are dealing with a possibility, not any kind of possibility, but something that is *within reach*. I have the

DOI: 10.4324/9781003124443-3

physical capability to go there, I have the money to pay for the ticket, it is OK for others for me to go (I am not supposed to take care of my child, for instance), I know the way to the theatre, etc. But despite all these things, I did not go. It was a possibility that did not actualize. What do we mean by this?

If this being-capable-of is not a physical fact or corporeal act, is it an imaginary one? Psychologism seems to be a natural alternative, but it will not do: I can imagine a lot of possibilities that are not within my reach (flying with my own wings, having been born to other parents, etc.), and I can also imagine something that I *think* are within my reach, but which are not. Being able to go to the movies is not an imaginary thing, it is something very real: that I can move, that I have enough money in my account, that I have no obligations for the night. It is not just possible, it is *potential*, a capacity (*dynamis* in Greek, *potentia* in Latin).

In addition to what we do, thus, we are surrounded by an infinite number of things that we did not do, do not do, or never will do. Our 'paths' as human beings are not simply a sequence of actual movements and locations following each other. We have behind us a number of possible events, and it makes perfect sense to consider what *would* have happened *if* we had done differently from what we did. These counterfactual clauses belong to the ones that only modal logic can deal with. Similarly, we have ahead of us a number of alternatives open to us, and we need to decide what to do.

But what is the ontology of these non-material objects (the one going to the movies) and non-material events? What makes them true, if they are real? The set-theoretical solution favoured by many philosophers is so-called possible worlds semantics. This means that, in addition to our actual world (what happens) we allow an infinite set on possible worlds, with their own inhabitants and features. Using these, we may say that even if I never went to the movies, *there is a possible world in which I did*. And since this is not the only thing I did not do even if I could have, there is an infinite set of possible worlds in which I *did* all these things. These possible worlds are what Jaakko Hintikka called *alternatives* (Hintikka, 1969). This happened long before so-called 'alternative facts' and should not be confused with them—although, paradoxically, there are always alternative facts, because we don't know everything. The alternative facts in Hintikka's sense are those that are compatible with what we know, not what we pretend to be facts.

The concept of an alternative can be used in all modal contexts. Since we don't know everything, our knowledge only rules out a subset of all possible worlds, leaving us with an infinite set of *epistemic alternatives*, those that we have to accept being possible, for all that we know. Similarly, what we believe forms a set of *doxastic alternatives* (worlds that are in accordance with what we believe), *perceptual alternatives* (those worlds that are in accordance with what we perceive), *mnemonic alternatives* (similarly related to our memory), and *deontic alternatives* (similarly related to our obligations). The inhabitants of these possible worlds are not the same as those in the actual world. For instance, I may mistakenly think that a man I see across the street is my former classmate. There must be a possible world, then, in which they *are* the same person. Hintikka even goes a step forward, concluding that we cannot start our understanding of the world from the actual world or the 'things' but rather from the set of all possible worlds, out of which we construct the world of things, by comparing their inhabitants. Those who show enough similarity and continuity can be called things.

I suppose that this already sounds like science-fiction, and I am not going to continue further along this route. But we could try to translate this into a more intuitive language. If we consider any 'thing' and claim to understand what it is, we have to understand not only what it is now but also what it can be. A cup can be in any location on the table, but it cannot float in the air or turn into a rabbit. Similarly, it is part of what I am that I can either stay at home or go to the movies. Thus, it is indeed similarity and continuity that we use as the criteria of being the same thing, and we see the possibilities 'within' things themselves, without being astonished when one of these possibilities becomes actual. 'In logic, nothing is accidental: if a thing can occur in an atomic fact, the possibility of that atomic fact must already be prejudged in the thing' (Wittgenstein, 1922, statement 2.012).

But the problem remains: even if we can 'see' (intuitively) what an object or a person can be or do, these powers cannot be observed in the same way as physical facts or events. One attempt to solve the problem is to zoom out, forgetting the individual and his idiosyncrasies. Even if the man did not actually go to the movies, many others did. This mass of people and its actual movement or flow is something that can be observed, giving us information on what kind of places attract people, how many people visit movie theatres and when, or what kind of routes they tend to take. This would, however, mean that instead of modalities, we would retreat back to actualities. The 'mass', the 'flow', and the 'stream' are mostly naturalistic metaphors—just like 'growth' discussed earlier—and they refer to something that does not exist as concrete thing or event, but which is abstracted from these concrete objects and events. Abstraction, on the other hand, is only possible by stripping from the concrete, material objects most of their attributes. The multitude of individual persons and their decisions are abstracted to an unconscious, unintentional flow of traffic, like a natural process based on gravitation.

But individuality is not the only thing that is lost along the modal concepts, but also space. Staying somewhere and moving along a path like a machine or stream is not yet space, at least not for us human beings. The crucial thing in the logic of modalities is that reality does not consist of only things in *stasis* or movement but also of possibilities and alternatives, in addition to what is or will ever be actualized. Reality is open, and the different alternatives it provides us make it meaningful. An urban square, for instance, is not only something that looks open space. If we take a photograph of it, we create an image that is no longer space, or at least not in the same sense than being physically present. Since it is public, or actually known by us to be public, we are free to choose whatever path and location that we like. Urban space is a space of alternatives, a modal space.

One could, of course, try to solve this by concentrating on the ability of the person, his access-ability, which refers to his potential or his strength to overcome the distances between locations. But even here we meet the necessity of abstraction: peoples' abilities, which are very different, (based on their physical strength or disabilities, their esteem, their wealth, and access to means of transport, etc.) and changing over time, which means that simply calculating the accessibility by car, by bicycle of by foot does not represent real access-ability, the potential to reach destinations. Furthermore, these abstractions usually disregard the other modal notions, such as knowledge, belief, fear, perception, memory, and permissibility. These concepts correspond to the epistemic, doxastic, perceived, mnemonic, and deontic alternatives.

Let us consider the square again. It is not enough to say that it is open, that is, not filled with buildings. Our individual has to know that it is open, where it is, how to get there, and what he can do there—public spaces are clearly not open for any kind of activities. It is even more important to know the possible uses of parks and urban forests. Some may be publicly owned and some not, there may be rules for public use of privately owned properties (e.g. everyman's right, right to roam). On the other hand, a foreigner may mistakenly believe that urban forests cannot be entered for picking berries and mushrooms, because they are privately owned, or even when they are owned by the city. The sets of doxastic and deontic alternatives thus intersect: there are permitted alternatives which are not believed to be permitted by our subject (in which case he is not capable to use them if he wants to obey the law or customs), and also those that are not permitted but believed to be permitted by him (in which case he easily runs into a conflict with others). Some of these conflicts are remembered by him, and he tries to avoid this kind of behaviour next time. Nevertheless, they remain as his mnemonic alternatives, the alternatives which are compatible with what he remembers. As we know, people may block certain painful experience from their memory, but this is not against the modal logic of memory; they simply do not belong to the mnemonic alternatives.

But this does not necessarily mean that fear would have disappeared. The difference between looking at pictures or wandering in virtual spaces and really being there, as a corporeal human being, is our vulnerability and mortality. You may die several times in a computer game but only once in real life. In life, *game over* really means game over, not square one. Feelings of security and feelings of fear are essential elements of our experience of urban spaces—and rural as well, as our popular movies of chainsaw massacres have taught us. Modalities are, thus, not only about what we can do but also what others can do to us, or what can happen to us. And in the long run, they are also about what can happen to our environment. Will my neighbourhood turn into a slum? Will the services of our town disappear? Will my children be safe?

Analysing multi-locality in terms of modalities gives us a somewhat different perspective from the traditional places-and-movements-between-them approach. Since being in a place means (unless one is incarcerated) the capability of not being there, leaving the place and entering another, this modality is already in this being-in-the-place. Therefore, one does not have to move cyclically between, for instance, one's apartment in the city and the second home in the countryside to be multi-local. Multi-locality is *within* him, mobility being real even if not actual. This is particularly evident if we do not reduce our discussion to residential multi-locality, which usually requires owning or renting two houses or apartment. Thus, we are approaching the understanding of many phenomena hitherto seen as 'normal' unilocality—such as commuting—as a form of multi-locality. One may own only one apartment but work in several places, one of them being one's home. In addition to the office, the library or the coffee shop can be used for working by her, and, thus, it is quite reasonable to call her multi-local. The point is that these are all available to her, included in her being.

This is probably what David Harvey had in mind when he introduced the concept relational space. This is how he defined it as part of his triad absolute-relative-relational:

> If we regard space as absolute it becomes a "thing in itself" with an existence independent of matter. It then possesses a structure which we can use to pigeon-hole or individuate phenomena. The view of relative space proposes that it be understood as a relationship between objects which exists only because objects exist and relate to each other. There is another sense in which space can be viewed as relative and I choose to call this relational space—space regarded in the manner of Leibniz, as being contained in objects in the sense that an object can be said to exist only insofar as it contains and represents within itself relationships to other objects.
>
> (Harvey, 2004)

One may of course wonder whether his concept of 'absolute space' is very useful, since the combination of Kantian *Ding-an-sich* with abstract and immaterial space, where (real) phenomena could still be located, is difficult to decipher. He also uses examples that further confuse us: 'The absolute conception may be perfectly adequate for issues of property boundaries and border determinations but it helps me not a whit with the question of what is Tiananmen Square or Ground Zero' (Harvey, 2004).

Privately owned land can indeed be measured and mapped, but it is only meaningful in relation to other private and public properties. It also has a political meaning, even though not as poignant than Tiananmen Square or Ground Zero. Owning a property means relative (not absolute) sovereignty over its use: one can build on one's land but only according to the zoning regulations. Some other people may also have a relative right to use it, as mentioned (e.g. everyman's right to roam). Thus, even if we can measure the distances and areas of one's property (or any other extension in the world), they can never be absolute. This measuring by land surveyors is itself a social and political practice. Referring to absolute space—or even relativity without social and political meaning—is thus hardly useful, since we are all the time dealing with what Harvey decided to call 'relational'.

The main question arising is, according to Harvey, 'how is it that different human practices create and make use of different conceptualizations of space' (Harvey, 2009). The official statistics can perhaps create 'containers' by the legislation requiring each person to register in one (and only one) address at a time. The social practices that families use to create their multi-local reality, on the other hand, are very different (Schier et al., 2015), and being private and social they defy political constructions of spatial relationships. These practices can be called 'placing' or 'home-making', consisting of several places, mobilities between them, social relations within them, and meanings generated by their use (Merriman, 2012).

Another theoretical attempt to include modalities in our environmental relationships is Gibson's theory of affordances (Gibson, 1986). It is an alternative to the mainstream theories of environmental perception, which are mainly directed as perception of things as they are (not as they can be). As mentioned, perception is one of the concepts that require modal operators in its logical analysis, since we can only perceive some things and not others (thus leaving other things open) but also because we often perceive incorrectly. If I am sure that I saw my friend in the crowd, then this possibility is clearly in accordance with my perception, even if it was actually another guy.

The concept of affordance means, according to Gibson, that as human animals we are not only perceiving things but directly what we can do with them, and what they can do to us (the cliff is climbable but it is also fall-off-able), that is, perceive directly their meaning and value (Gibson, 1986). These affordances are relatively stable, since they have developed in our evolution to enable us to survive in our ecological niche. There are problems in this conceptual framework, however, since people's abilities to act in their environment are highly context-dependent (Chemero & Turvey, 2007; Scarantino, 2003). According to Shaw et al. (2019), this problem can be solved by interpreting affordances as types, which could then be perceived as abstract types instead of tokens (concrete instantiations) which can be seen. One can ask, however, whether we can talk about perception anymore with such abstractions (and not, for instance, understanding or constructing).

Another problem is that as Gibson is mainly discussing human beings as an animal-species, the concept of affordance is hardly very useful in characterizing our perception of cultural values. If you consider an urban environment, one needs to have a lot of cultural literacy even to survive there (something that cannot have developed through evolution), to say nothing of perceiving the value and meaning of a work of art or architecture. In the institutional context, a planner needs to be able to see the potential of a city, a neighbourhood or un urban block, and this ability can only have developed through proper education and experience.

Without going further into this debate in ecological psychology, it can clearly be seen that the ontology of modal notions is challenging in specialized sciences. Since the possibilities are not based on psychology (imagination), and since we cannot 'go through' all the possible worlds that our perception, beliefs, or knowledge allow us, we need to see the 'strength' or 'potential' in what we meet or consider. This is what Jonathan Jacobs wanted to do with his 'powers theory', rejecting the dominant paradigm of possible worlds (Jacobs, 2010). In a way, he had the same intention as I did above, trying to describe modal logic in a more 'intuitive' way.

Let us consider once more the opening sentence of this chapter. Why can we see from the modal operator 'could have gone' that it is happening in an urban context? The corresponding descriptive sentences 'I went to the movies' and 'I stayed at home' (which can both be true but not at the same time, unlike the modal sentence) do not include such a connotation. Of course, such descriptive sentences can be found, like 'I stopped in a couple of bars and had a beer on my way home'—living in the village you are lucky to have one bar. Both are, however, related to accessibility, reachability, something that is there even if we would choose not to use them.

How would urbanity and urbanization turn out if we would use the modal logic and ontology described above, instead of the usual numbers and growth of people (i.e. state-people) in specified geographical territories? As we can clearly see, the sentences reveal urbanity through reachability. And if the movie theatres and bars are reachable (when they are close enough), second homes, other cities, coworking spaces, and holiday resorts are also reachable, even if they are not close by, with faster transportation and communication technologies, as well as new organizational principles that give more degrees of freedom. This reachability and accessibility seem to be the key in understanding urbanity, if we give up the traditional way of discussing urbanization through non-existent abstract state-people.

4 Multi-locality as urbanization

As one reads articles and books on urbanization, it does not take long before the authors turn to *data*. Even before analysing what urbanization might be, the scholars start to measure it. We already discussed this in the introduction, but let us return to it in more detail, since this *data-drivenness* is so characteristic of contemporary studies on urbanization. Consider the following dictionary definition of urbanization by Ray Hutchison (Hutchison, 2010, pp. 886–887):

> Urban studies is commonly divided into two subject areas: urbanism (the study of urban life, or the impact of cities upon human behavior) and urbanization (the study of the growth of cities). Urbanization further includes the process of population concentration within human settlements (the city), as well as the expansion of cities into surrounding communities (suburbanization) and regions.

This definition seems quite plausible, but it already contains words like 'growth', 'population', 'concentration', 'settlement', 'expansion', 'community', and 'region', which sound innocent when you first see them, but which become very complicated when you start scrutinizing them. What is 'growth' if it is not growth? What is 'population' if it is not people? What is 'population concentration' if it is not concentration of people in a certain place at a certain time? What is 'expansion into communities'. Does it contain second home owners in a rural community? Or tourists visiting local communities? If not, why not? Are these not particularly urban phenomena, very different from the cultures and practices of traditional rural communities?

Questions like this are usually not asked, but this does not prevent scholars from declaring *how many* people there are, or have been, in different cities. As mentioned in the introduction, we have heard hundreds of times that more than half of the world population now *live* in urban areas, even though there were only 12% of them in the beginning of the twentieth century. We have followed the 'growth' of individual cities and their changing positions in the hierarchy of world cities. We have compared the

DOI: 10.4324/9781003124443-4

urbanization following the industrial revolution to urban growth in the contemporary developing countries (Jedwah et al., 2017), being assured that we are talking about the same phenomenon.

Consider the following introduction in Jedwah et al.'s paper on demography, urbanization, and development (2017, p. 6):

> Urban expansion in the developing world has been dramatic. Between 1950 and 2015, the total urban population in developing countries increased tenfold from about 300 million to 3 billion; the urban share tripled from about 17% to 50% (United Nations, 2013).

We have not heard definitions of 'urban expansion', 'total urban population', or 'urban share', but that does not prevent the authors from giving exact data on them, referring to the same authoritative source that we already found problematic. 'Urban share' or 'urban population' doesn't make much sense if people are constantly on the move, both in the cities and in the countryside, as well as between them. Even if land-use could be divided into urban and non-urban (which is in itself arbitrary), people cannot.

The problem is that data are by no means natural. They may be connected to natural phenomena (bodies, vegetation, water), but in order to become data they need to be artificially constructed and collected. In this process, they may even lose the connection to natural phenomena that they perhaps once had. If national governments politically decide that you can only have one permanent or temporary residence at a time, and that this permanent address is based on your own reporting to the national registry, then this data (from which the 'urban population', 'rural population', and 'urban share' are drawn) has lost its connections to the corporeal people and their whereabouts. If, additionally, the supreme administrative court decides that it doesn't matter how many nights you spend in which location (such a ruling has indeed been made in Finland), then the 'living' that we are talking about in the context of urbanization has nothing to do with living.

On the other hand, we know that people have always come to the cities to sell their goods, or that they have left the cities to sell their products in other cities and countries. People have come to the cities for work or for cultural activities. They have left the cities for grand tours, for crusades, or for business trips. They have cruised around the world in huge passenger boats, of the size of small towns. Considering all this, does it rather seem that *this* is what urbanity is all about, *movement* that never stops? Why, then, do we want to find a certain *number* of people to characterize a city, as if they did not move, as if they would *stay*? Furthermore, this number is not the number of people inside the city at any given time, if we would take a snapshot of the city. The vendors in the market square are not counted, nor the tourists sightseeing or staying in hotels, or those in the cruise ships. In contrast, those who would be travelling or spending time in their second home *are* counted.

No wonder that mainstream urban studies have had a hard time trying to understand multi-locality, which is exactly this: *movement* and *modalities*.

This phenomenon—data coming before concepts—could be compared to what is called 'quantified self', people constructing their self or identity by collecting data of themselves with smartphones, activity bracelets, smartwatches, or rings: steps taken every day, hours and quality of sleep, heartbeats, blood pressure, calories consumed, etc. They do not start by considering something that is important to them—such as health—by analysing what it means and how it could be measured. They simply start collecting data, and as you have it, you can start playing with it. This is called *data fetishism*: a belief that quantified data has by itself an aura of objectivity, even if, for example, measuring your movements during the night is not a very reliable measure of the quality of sleep. Tamar Sharon and Dorien Zandbergen argue that data fetishism is only a part of quantifying selves, it can also be a practice of mindfulness, resistance, or communicative and narrative practice (Sharon & Zandbergen, 2017). Be that as it may for individual persons, but the same practice in urban studies on the city apparently has no such psychological dimension—particularly not resistance—but the aura of objectivity is clearly there, much earlier than an eventual analysis of the main questions, such as living, staying, residing, place, or space. Even more than this: the analysis may never appear, not even the basic distinction between being a corporeal human being and being registered to a certain address.

As artefacts, data are measured in a chosen way, they are gathered, they are stored, and they are manipulated. They are no more nor less real than, say, stories. And indeed, you can tell stories with data with an 'aura of objectivity'. Let us return to the famous storyteller, Edward Glaeser, the title of whose book we discussed earlier. This is how he puts data to work in his narrative, in a not too uncommon argument:

> There is a near-perfect correlation between urbanization and prosperity across nations. On average, as the share of a country's population that is urban rises by 10 percent, the country's per capita output increases by 30 percent. Per capita incomes are almost four times higher in those countries where a majority of people live in cities than in those countries where a majority of people live in rural areas.
>
> (Glaeser, 2011, p. 7)

Those of us who have been sitting in methodology classes in universities have been warned of confusing correlation with causality. The amount of ice-cream sold correlates heavily with the number of people drowning, but people don't drown in ice-cream. Glaeser is clever enough not to mention causality, but he does conclude—in the next paragraph— that 'cities enhance prosperity'. A responsible researcher takes correlation only as a starting point: it tells us something, but what? Clearly the ice-cream–drowning–correlation has causally something to do with the summer and high temperatures, but what about cities?

Implicit causality is not, however, the only problem in the story of the 'triumph of the city'. Glaeser uses concepts like 'population that is urban', 'living in cities', and 'living in countryside'. As we have seen, these are not unambiguous concepts. In order to compare the 'share of a country's population that is urban' with the corresponding share of the country's population that is 'rural', one would have to be able to divide the population into two groups, urban and rural. But this is exactly something that you cannot do. Even those who only have one address may live in suburbs, exurbs and in the countryside where they have built there one-family houses, commuting daily to the city. Are they urban or rural, living in the country but working in the city? And consider again the man who has an apartment in the city but a house in the countryside, where his wife lives, and where he spends his weekends and occasionally teleworks—until the pandemic has forced him to full-time teleworking, and he has given up his city apartment until he again needs it. Is he urban or rural? Or was he urban when he still had the apartment in the city but rural when he gave it away? Doesn't earning your salary from the city count as urban? And if not, what counts? We clearly have no answers to these questions, but we do have *data*. We are indeed *data-driven*.

'City', as well as 'urban' and 'rural', are of course abstract concepts, and in a flat ontology they cannot causally influence anything. We should beware of *reification* of abstract concepts and think instead by what causal chains we could suppose that people 'living in cities' become more prosperous, as Glaeser suggests. This is how the story unfolds in the city of Athens, according to him:

> Athens grew by trading wine, olive oil, spices, and papyrus [...] Athens pulled in the best minds of battle-scarred Asia Minor. Hippodamus came from Miletus to plan the city's harbour. Others came to tutor wealthy Athenians. This first generation of Athenian scholars then influenced their friends and students, like Pericles and Socrates. Socrates generated his own innovations and taught Plato, who taught Aristotle./This remarkable period saw the birth of not only Western philosophy but also of drama and history, as artists and scholars from all over the Mediterranean world converged in a single spot that gave them the proximity and the freedom to share their ideas. Athens flowered because of small random events that then multiplied through urban interaction. One smart person met another and sparked a new idea. That idea inspired someone else, and all of a sudden something really important had occurred. The ultimate cause of Athenian success may seem mysterious, but the process is clear. Ideas move from person to person within dense urban spaces, and this exchange occasionally creates miracles of human creativity.
>
> (ibid., p. 19)

I needed to quote this at length, because the two paragraphs contain an important feature of urbanity—connections—but, at the same time, a very questionable explanation of why cities flourish: random encounters and dense urban spaces. Keep in mind that there really is correlation between these features, but that correlation does not entail causality. The story starts with Athenian trading, which created the material conditions for the flourishing of philosophy and the arts. This was not merely internal, but the trade routes extended to the whole Mediterranean world, which required ship-building and seafaring skills. Thus, connections to the market. The development of philosophy and the arts also required connections between scholars and artists, including the most important teacher-student-connections from Socrates to Plato to Aristotle, the three men who established the basic elements of Western thought. Thus, connections to talent and wisdom. But randomness? And dense urban spaces? Where do they come in? Are we supposed to believe that Plato randomly met Socrates and started to develop some new ideas? Or should we rather say that they were student and teacher, they sought out each other? Socrates was known to be 'the wisest man alive', and thus it made sense for the young students to seek his company, just like contemporary students seek famous professors to tutor them. This is not randomness, it is intentionality.

Let us consider another story—a true story this time, unlike the story of Plato running into Socrates—of a success story of a group of eight students in the Finnish city of Tampere. They were selected to study architecture at the local university of technology, and there they met each other. While they were preparing their school assignments, they rented a common office for working and giving peer support to each other. Having learned how to work together, they started taking part in open architectural competitions, and eventually became very successful in them. One year, they won every single competition in the country, except for one in which they had not submitted an entry. As real design commissions started to pour in, they established an architectural office called '8-studio' and were able to hire colleagues and younger students. As many of their customers were in the capital region, the office was split into two, half of them moving to Helsinki. As the founding members of the office aged, some of them also became professors, educating the younger generation of architecture students.

The things that made the success story did not include randomness or density. They did not run into each other, they all wanted to become successful architects, perhaps even 'starchitects'. They were talented enough to be selected to the university, and there they were able to get to know each other and each other's skills and working practices. They selected the classmates they wanted to work with and learned from each other's work. The common mistake in urban stories is to assume that events like this would be random, since they were not part of the curriculum or a personal plan. But this was not a random event of 'one smart person meeting another and sparking a new idea'. They intentionally sought to study architecture, and you can only study architecture in a few universities (in Finland, only three), and they happen to be in major cities. No one could have known beforehand that exactly this group of eight would become successful, but it was much more *probable* that they would find each other among their classmates than running into them on the street, no matter how big or dense the city would be.

A similar probability is the reason why researchers go to international conferences to meet their colleagues, listen to the latest research results, and network with interesting people. It might seem that some of the encounters happen randomly, but planning theorists don't go to dentists' conferences or ask people over the street if they are interested in a selected topic. They intentionally go to events where the *probability* to find interesting colleagues is highest. Even if they live in a big city, they will not find the most interesting people working on their subject there, let alone randomly—that is why they go to *international* conferences.

Thus, the moral of the story—and a potential explanation of the success of people in the cities—seems to be connectedness, not randomness generated by a big city, nor density of its population (how many people are registered close to each other). But the obvious counter-argument is, of course, that these connections cannot exist without a big city, and such cities tend to be densely populated, at least in their centres, compared to the surrounding countryside and smaller towns. There can only be universities in cities, and talent is concentrated in cities. In addition to universities, high quality services in general can only exist in big cities, since only there they have the necessary customer base. Indeed, connections to the customers are essential for businesses to thrive.

But it would be a mistake to suppose that the city, even if it were a megacity, could succeed in the globalized world without connections to other cities and countries. A good theatre is visited by spectators from the surrounding regions and even from other countries. A good university is dependent on a continuous exchange of students, teachers and researchers. And a global company, of course, needs connections to its customers but also sub-contractors all over the world. When the pandemic hit, conferences and business trips were cancelled or went online, hotels in big cities stood empty, and the tourism industry was choking. The manufacturing industries were suffering from their broken global production chains. 'If I have 49 parts of the 50 that I need to make a bicycle, I will not produce any bicycle', one producer complained. These types on connections—within and beyond the city borders—are of course mixed, and they support each other: a businessman travelling to meet a client in another country does not need the density of his neighbourhood to succeed in his business, but he does need taxi services between his home or office and the airport, as well as restaurants where he might like to meet his client. Local services are useful to him, and they need local density to survive.

But let us make a thought experiment—unrealistic in this one case. What if we could have all the connections that the city can provide *without* the crowd that they usually require? Forget that it is impossible, imagine it just for the sake of argument. We would still have the good restaurants, and we would always find a table. We could always get a ticket to a concert or sports event. There would not be much traffic, no noise and clean air. There would be plenty of shops and other services. The taxi would not get stuck in a traffic jam, and there would be no queues at the airport. There would also be an extensive amount of green in the city for recreational purposes. Nevertheless, we would still be able to meet the people who we really want to meet. Would such a city be an ideal living environment?

Partly yes, if we believe the results of studies on housing preferences. In a recent survey in Finland, the respondents were asked to mention three most important positive and negative features of their neighbourhood (Strandell, 2017). Number one was the location and connections (54%), the second and third place were given to a natural environment (44%) and calmness (42%)—not very urban features. Density itself was marginal as a positive feature, only 0.6% mentioned it. On the other hand, 10% mentioned it as a negative feature in their neighbourhood. Could we conclude, thus, that density and its discontents (noise, pollution, unsafety, social unrest, crowds, traffic jams) are not a positive feature of living in the city, but *collateral damage*, the price that has to be paid for the connections (that determine the location) and accessibility to a variety of services and jobs.

Our thought-experiment is of course impossible, not only economically but also socially, since a city with all the services but few people would not produce the anonymity that big cities are famous for, and which can also be experienced as a positive and essential feature of urbanity. Being in the crowd means that you are among a lot of people you don't know, and consequently you don't need to react to their presence, unless there is some specific reason for that. There is a sort of freedom in being unknown, the ability to be by yourself among the crowd of other people. The famous metropolitan mentality analysed by Simmel has its negative features (blasé attitude, rationality in social relationships, money as the dominant value), but the resulting anonymity also creates a personal space quite unlike the one that you have among the people you know.

What would it mean if we tried to theorize urbanization not in terms of size, density, growth, or the share of urban and rural population, but in terms of connections? Connections in this context does not refer to flows of information, things or people, but potential encounters between people, things, and spaces. The difficulties of mainstream urban studies in dealing with multi-locality has to do with confusing actuality (what actually happens) with potentiality (what can happen, what can be done). Staying in one place, for a shorter or longer time, means at the same time that there are several potential places that can be entered, with the social and economic potential that they offer.

Thus, one should not assume that the 'metropolitan mentality' that Simmel describes is the mentality of any one person. Rather it is the social context that those entering the city need to learn, the rules of conduct one needs to follow in order to survive in an urban context. Changing this context into a suburban subdivision, a small town, or a rural village, requires adjustment, perhaps even daily or weekly if you are living a multi-local life. In Vittorio Sica's film *Miracle in Milan* (1951) the protagonist is leaving the orphanage where he has spent his youth, after losing his foster grandmother in a rural village. He starts greeting complete strangers whom he meets on the street, raising ignorance, astonishment, and even aggression. In a big city, this is out of place, unlike in the countryside where he had spent his childhood. Immobility (incarceration) does not require adjustment.

If connections would be understood as the defining feature of urbanity (and size and density of population as its by-products, collateral damage, or even artificial constructs), we naturally need to consider the role of the ICT that has made multi-locality so much easier and revolutionized the spatial relationships between people and places. This has happened so fast that our language and thought have had difficulties in accommodating to it. We are still accustomed to thinking that we are at a certain place at a certain time, and that we are then absent from all other places. Even the landline telephone did not challenge this understanding, since we were calling *from* somewhere *to* another place, and the caller and the receiver of the call were clearly located. But as mobile devices and wi-fi-networks have become ubiquitous, the location has lost part of its relevance. If I send or receive an e-mail, it does not matter *where* my colleague sends or receives it, only that he does. If I need to reach someone by phone, I usually don't need to think *where* she is. I may ask whether she has *time* to talk to me, but this time does not have a place. The same is true of her, she does not need to consider my whereabouts. The situation may change, of course. If I have arranged to meet a friend at a certain place at a certain time and she does not show up, I may call her and ask 'Where are you?'— this *where* meaning, actually, '*not here*' or '*how far from here*', or '*why are you not here?*'

As the pandemic forced workers and students to work online, an interesting social experiment followed. Many people opened a window to their private realm, letting their colleagues to see the interior of their apartments and listen to the noise of their children or the barking of their dogs. Others were careful to close their cameras and microphones whenever possible and used background images, raising their faces again at the centre of attention. Thus, there emerged a mixture of public and private spaces, as well as places and placelessness. Probably the software used for teleconferencing will develop substantially in the future, but the main issue remains. Where am I? Where is she? Am I there, intruding into her private space? Or is she here, as if discussing in my living room? Or is there a space between our two places where we meet? If we are offered a virtual meeting room where our avatars can discuss 'around a table' as we used to do in our former life, there will still be a mixture of public and private, as I am aware of my existence in both the physical and the virtual space.

People have always dreamed of being in other places and travelled to them in their imagination ('I'll be home for Christmas, if only in my dreams'). The ubiquity of ICT has, however, brought this simultaneous being-here and being-there as an everyday form of existence. It has meant a dramatic change in the dominance of proximity and contiguity and, consequently, the possibility of several types of geographical constellations of living. We are often reminded, however, that the 'weakening' or even 'disappearing' of distances has not resulted in a dispersal of living arrangements or economic activities: cities are still 'growing' and, interestingly, the high-tech companies tend to prefer central locations. But we should perhaps be careful not to draw too hasty conclusions. It is clear that virtual connections do not replace face-to-face encounters, and the possibility to telework does not mean that people would 'move back to the countryside'. But something is obviously happening, and we don't have enough experience to know where it leads us.

Let us again consider a story, this time of a young PhD student who was preparing his dissertation in the early 1990s, while working in a small city of 70 000 inhabitants to earn his living. It soon became clear that the city was too small for him. Even though there was a small university, his field of research was not represented. The bookshops in the city did not sell academic books, and the university libraries that he would have needed were in bigger cities. He could use interlibrary loans, but they were expensive for a poor student, and in any case, he would have had to visit the libraries to know which books are available (the internet did not yet provide this information). Additionally, he had to visit a bigger city to discuss with his tutor. Life would have been much easier if he had found a job in a bigger city. Nevertheless, he managed to graduate, moved to a bigger city and finally got a job in the metropolitan area.

Thirty years later, he was living in a small village of only 800 inhabitants. Things were, however, quite different. Sitting in his study by his computer he could do most of his work: have meetings, give lectures and seminars, tutor his PhD students, and write publications with colleagues in Oslo and Vienna. He could read scientific journals and e-books with his tablet or e-book reader. He could buy everything he needed from the largest online shops in the world, including the books he needed. Even groceries could be ordered to his doorstep. Paradoxically, what had actually happened was that the capital city of his country had already become too small. Its 'academic' bookshop was not so academic anymore, since it could not compete with Amazon and had to concentrate on bestsellers and life-coaching, just like the bookshops in the small town. His colleagues were working in universities around the world, not even in his native country. After work, he could watch films streamed to his devices or read novels with his e-book reader. Paradoxically, even though there was only a small village around him, there was actually a whole 'city' at his fingertips.

It is clear that he could not have foreseen all this in the early 1990s, having just abandoned his typewriter and started using his first computer for text-processing. But he was not the only one. One of the most famous scholars writing on the emerging 'network society' is Manuel Castells, whose terms 'space of flows and 'space of places' I shall discuss in a moment. In the second edition of his seminal work *The Rise of the Network Society* from 2000, he tried to foresee the spatial impacts of the new technology connecting people through computer networks. Obviously, most of the everyday functions had already had a taste of the network society: work, shopping, entertainment, health care, education, public services, and governance. But what would actually change?

> A dramatic increase of teleworking is the most usual assumption about the impact of information technology on cities, and the last hope for metropolitan transport planners before surrendering to the inevitability of the mega-gridlock. Yet, in 1988, a leading European researcher on telecommuting could write, without the shadow of a joke, that 'there are more people doing research on telework than there are actual teleworkers' – – telecommuters *stricto sensu* employed regularly to work on-line at home, is very small overall and *is not expected to grow substantially in the foreseeable future.*
>
> (Castells, 2000, my italics)

That was in 2000, and obviously the foreseeable future did not extend to the year 2020. Before the pandemic, the incidence of regular or occasional teleworking (home-based and mobile telework combined) varied from 30% in Denmark, the Netherlands and Sweden to 10% in the Mediterranean countries, and just 2% in Argentina (ILO, 2021). When the pandemic hit and governments started to take action, almost 34% of employees in European Union started teleworking. In Finland, almost 60% started teleworking from home, and this figure does not include the schoolchildren and students who were also sent home to study (ILO, 2021, p. 4). Obviously, these figures will not last when (or if) the situation is normalized, but both employers and employees are now reflecting on new forms of hybrid working, combining face-to-face and online activities. Why should employers pay high rents for large traditional office spaces if work gets done anyway? Why should employees waste time and money in commuting to work every morning?

But what about teleshopping?

> Teleshopping was slow to live up to its promise, and ultimately was pushed out by the Internet's competition. It supplemented rather than replaced commercial areas. However, e-commerce, with billions of dollars of on-line sales in the US over Christmas 1999, is a major, new development. Nevertheless, the growing importance of online transactions does not imply the disappearance of shopping centers and retail stores. In fact, the trend is the opposite: shopping areas proliferate around the urban and suburban landscape, with showrooms that address customers to on-line ordering terminals to get the actual goods, often home-delivered.
>
> (Castells, 2000, pp. 426–427)

When Castells started writing his book in 1996, Amazon had been established as an online bookshop two years earlier. In 2021, it sells everything under the sun, for the staggering sum of 21.33 billion in 2020. And it is not the only one: the global retail sales were up to 4.28 trillion US dollars. It is obvious that the 'showroom' strategy with 'ordering terminals' did not materialize, and online shopping is really challenging traditional shopping centres and retail stores, particularly the small corner shops that New Urbanists hope to save our cities.

Nevertheless, of course, the shopping centres did not disappear. The same observations can be made of the banking services. Castells assumed that even though banks are interested in eliminating branch offices and replacing them by online services, 'the consolidated bank branches continue as service centres, to sell financial products to their customers through a personalized relationship'. He even told a funny story of a telephone banking branch that considered it necessary to be located in Leeds in order to service its customers in West Yorkshire's plain accent (ibid., p. 427). Again, local branch offices did not totally disappear, and in smaller places one can still have a personal relationship with your bank manager, but the number of the offices has been substantially reduced, at the same time as most of the services can be reached online: receiving your salary, paying your bills, doing your savings and investments, and even applying for a bank loan. You perhaps still need to visit the office to sign eventual contracts, but even this is turning digital.

In fact, there are two common mistakes that we often hear in the connection of telework, teleshopping, telebanking, etc. One is the imagination that we could foresee what is coming to us with new technology and what are its social and spatial impacts. The other is the denial of the 'death of the city' as the result of the disappearing distances and the diminished role of proximity and contiguity. There is an inherent tendency to 'traditionalize' our thinking even on the impacts of new technology: if teleworking is marginal today, it must be marginal tomorrow. If people are not interested in teleshopping today, why would they be tomorrow? Second, we make the logical mistake of confusing what is possible with what is or what will happen. Indeed, Castells was right in his argument that teleshopping is supplementary: it is a new potentiality, not a replacement. The fear (or the dream) of the city disappearing is, thus, based on the false assumption that there is an inherent ideal spatial preference of human beings, and it is to stay home, as far from other people as possible. Being 'locked' at home is not, however, our foremost intention or dream. To the contrary, we want to be free to move, and this is why mobile technologies and networks are so relevant to our spatial organization. And this is why cities as nodal points are so important also in the future, despite the *possibility* to avoid them.

But even though cities will not disappear, what will they be like? As I have been arguing throughout this book, the dichotomies urban/non-urban or city/countryside are misleading and also lead us to the false conclusion that multi-locality, as living and working in several places and landscapes, would somehow be an *opposite* or a *challenge* to urbanization. If urbanization is understood as the growth of cities (more people 'moving to urban areas'), it entails the acceptance of this dichotomy. Medieval cities still had walls around them with gates as the only entrance points, which made it possible to say whether you were inside or outside the city. But even these cities 'inhaled': peasants and vendors arrived every morning, and ships sailed to other cities to sell their products. In the contemporary city, the city walls have been demolished and, perhaps, transformed into ring roads as in Vienna. The only replacement of the city wall is the administrative border, still defining the city as a political community. Those registered inside the administrative area pay taxes to the municipality, receive its services and can vote in local elections. As communities, however, big cities are 'imagined' in much the same way as nations, as Anderson argued (Anderson, 2006), and for the users of the city these borders are absolutely permeable.

If we would say that the city ends where its administrative area ends, we would be talking about a political entity of local sovereignty. It can be clearly delineated, but it is not a city of people, not is it a cultural phenomenon. We cannot suppose that corporeal people crossing the administrative borders would suddenly become rural or adopt a non-urban lifestyle. But how far do they have to go to be outside the urban? There are attempts to define concepts that would better correspond to the actual use of cities than the administrative entity, such as 'functional city-region'. Nevertheless, as Davoudi and Brooks have argued (Davoudi & Brooks, 2020), the borders of such city-regions are arbitrary, and they are even less cultural or even political. There are regional authorities in many countries, but, as we noticed, corporeal people easily cross not only regional but also national borders. But if we cannot put an end to the city, is it losing its meaning altogether? This has indeed raised some fears. Some urban activists have attempted to 'retake' urbanity by redefining it as the traditional, dense urban structure, with corner shops and cafeterias, in a 'fifteen minutes city' where everything you need would be within walking or cycling distance or within the reach of public transport. However, as we noticed, you can have 'everything you need' even within half a minute's distance, without any need for urban density or using public transportation. On the other hand, if it is Rome, New York, or Tokyo where you want to go to spend time, or where you need to go for your business purposes, no density or public transportation in your own city will allow you to reach them in 15 minutes. What you need is an airport and good airline services. In other words, connections.

Should we then say that urbanization is best understood at the planetary scale? This is indeed the conclusion that many scholars have reached. The term 'planetary urbanization' was introduced by Henri Lefebvre in his book *The Urban Revolution* (1970), and it has subsequently been debated (e.g. Castells, 1977 Brenner, 2018; Merrifield, 2013). If our contemporary urban reality is based on a network of global cities as command- and control centres of the world economy, these nodal points are already *conceptually* dependent on the several other places that they control. They can only *exist* as nodal points.

Let us consider this idea more closely. If we need to give up the traditional understanding of cities as areas with certain characteristics, such as density or the number of registered persons and businesses, what kind of entity are we talking about? If it does not have a borderline or territory, allowing us to say whether someone or something is inside or outside the city, we need to make a conceptual turn. Lefebvre's solution was to move from cities to what he called *urban society* and its hypothetical end-point, *complete urbanization*. This would make it possible to conceptualize urban and urbanization as a process—not a process of more and more people 'moving' to the city, but a cultural and economic process. He traces the development of the urban society as a series of discontinuous transformations from the political city of administration and power to the mercantile city and to the industrial city. The key change in these transformations was that the city shifted its shape from an isolated and contained centre to what industrialization led us, *implosion-explosion*: simultaneous urban concentration, rural exodus, extension of the urban fabric, and complete subordination of the agrarian to the urban (Lefebvre, 2003).

In this way, searching for the borders of the city in vain poses no problem for us, since urban society extends everywhere on the planet. Human activities, buildings and wealth concentrate in global cities and smaller cities and towns, but it would be myopic to concentrate only on what happens in these centres. There cannot be a centre without a periphery, and what happens in the periphery is also part of urbanization. This includes suburbs and exurbs, the surrounding rural municipalities from which people commute to work in the city, the large infrastructures built around cities, and even the vacation homes. These have essential connections to cities—they could not be thought without them. On the other hand, they can have very loose connections to their immediate surroundings. Agriculture that used to be the main means of living in the countryside has been transformed into industrial farming with larger estates, more machines and less farmers. Professional fishing that used to keep island communities alive has disappeared, but the islands are not empty: they are filled with vacation houses that often have very little to do with the surrounding political community or even the local economy, apart from occasional visits to the local shops.

This interpretation of the urban fabric and urban society gives us a natural explanation of why multi-locality has become such a growing phenomenon. It has nothing to do with 'returning to the countryside' or 'counter-urbanization'. It has a cultural and social meaning in addition to the physical structures in the landscape, and it has a clear connection to the forms of production and the corresponding rhythms of it. The industrial city created the man-machine-relationship and the necessary temporal and spatial contiguity of industrial production, resulting in both alienation from the product of labour and the daily, weekly, and yearly rhythm of work and leisure. Weekends and holidays combined with the spread of the private car made possible the most traditional and most wide-spread form of multi-locality, that of second homes. As the forms of production are changing into more information-intensive industries and, thus, becoming more place-independent, the dichotomy between 'permanent' home and 'vacation house' has become outdated. But the work done in the former vacation house—current second home—is no more connected to the immediate surroundings than leisure was. What has become essential is a fast internet connection to the world outside. Computer networks have replaced fishing nets.

This brings us back to Castells' network society and his space of flows. As we are no longer dealing with natural flows (for the fishermen), nor flows of things (for the consumers), but virtual networks, I am not sure whether the metaphor of flow is the best one to describe what is actually happening in these networks—and definitely not what is potentially happening in them. A natural flow is a thing, albeit a moving thing. It is not human, and thus it has no plans or intentionality—something that we found essential in urbanity (in Chapter 3). It has no direction of its own, but its movement is totally dictated by the topography of the terrain. And it cannot not-flow, which is an essential part of human modalities. We can download information from a website and, as a result, information 'flows' from a server to our computer. But we can also choose not to, and perhaps choose another site. Perhaps we cannot find the information we search because we don't know where to look for (the site does not belong to our 'epistemic alternatives'). Or perhaps downloading this information is illegal (i.e. it does not belong to our 'deontic alternatives'). It is a good thing, indeed, that information is not simply 'flowing' in.

It is illustrative to compare this with the pre-digital era when information was transferred through letters and other slow media. Castells referred to a study from 1990 by Michelson and Wheeler on the data traffic by Federal Express Corporation—overnight letters, packages, and boxes between US metropolitan areas as well as international destinations. In this context, the concept of flow did make some sense: letters and packages were 'flowing' from one sender to one destination. But even then, one could decide whether to send the letter and what information to include in it. Unlike a flowing river, human beings are intentional. The receivers of the information were also dependent on the senders and what was intentionally sent to them. If they wanted to get information that was not directly available, they had to go to libraries or archives, and these were concentrated in the major cities. Information sharing and searching in the contemporary information society may technically look similar (and the major urban hubs are the same), but the nodes are more dispersed (every home that is connected to the internet is a university library), and working in the information space is socially and culturally different from sending and receiving letters. The spatial implications are evident. If in Hägerstrand's time-geography one needed to have a fixed, physical address to receive messages, today's nomad worker does not need such a 'homebase'. It is also important to see that, unlike Castells saw in 2000, telecommuters *stricto sensu* are no longer 'employed regularly to work on-line at home'. Home is only one of the places where 'telecommuters' work, since wi-fi's and 4G or 5G networks are almost everywhere. They offer a huge number of potential workplaces, of which the office can still be one. And if there are several homes, home is not a place anymore, it is rather a process of home-making (Schier et al., 2015).

Thus, the metaphor of flow is problematic because it lacks the dimension of modalities: the potentialities based on the knowledge, beliefs, perceptions, memories, and normative requirements of the subject. On the other hand, there is another problem with the concept of the space of flows and its opposite, the space of places. This is the persistent dualism in our traditional conceptual frameworks trying to deal with contemporary urban society. As discussed in the introduction, the concepts of urban and rural lead to paradoxes, since it is impossible to draw the line after which the man travelling to his second home would cease to be urban and become rural. Similar problems are implied by Tuan's dichotomy between space and place. One may ask, thus, whether the concepts 'space of flows' and 'space of places' were an offspring of the same dominant Western dualism.

Consider the way that Castells defined a place: 'A place is a locale whose form, function, and meaning are self-contained within the boundaries of physical contiguity'. However, this would entail that there are no places, since it is impossible to imagine a place that would be so 'self-contained', including the Parisian quartier of Belleville that he uses as his example. The connections that add to the potentialities of any place necessarily change its function and meaning, which are no longer based on physical contiguity—or actually never were. And Castells was well aware of that: '[...] people still live in places. But because function and power in our societies are organised in the space of flows, the structural domination of its logic essentially alters the meaning and dynamic of places' (Castells, 2000, p. 458).

We may interpret this paradox in various ways. It can be seen as a dialectical process between two inconsistent opposites, the self-contained place or container and the growing dominance of the space of flows: 'The dominant tendency is toward a horizon of networked, ahistorical space of flows, aiming at imposing its logic over scattered, segmented places, increasingly unrelated to each other, less and less able to share cultural codes'. (ibid., p. 459). Dialectics notwithstanding, it still seems difficult to cope with the underlying dualism, since how can these fragmented places be increasingly unrelated to each other *at the same time* as the networks become stronger? How can they be less and less able to share cultural codes if teleworkers are writing codes in their apartments and sharing them with their employers in other continents? Are these computer codes not cultural, in the same sense as the habits of greeting (or not greeting) your neighbours when you see them? Are they not historical, even though we could not imagine them 50 years ago, and we cannot imagine what they will be 50 years from now?

Another possible interpretation could be that the place as defined by Castells is not a real but ideological place, or place as defined by ideology. At the same time as ICT is shortening distances or even making them irrelevant compared to connections, we still meet images of contiguity that have also found their way into planning. At the same time as cities are 'growing', the small community of neighbours has retained its normative power. If staying 'rooted' in one place is normatively superior to moving, or moving shorter distances within a contained community superior to intercontinental mobility, an 'urban village', seems to be the normative ideal. One recent planning concept is indeed called 'the fifteen minutes city': you should be able to reach everything you need within 15 minutes of walking, cycling, or using public transport—that is, staying close. This requires—and legitimizes—a compact city, which is also in the interests of developers in the growing metropolises. Thus, it seems that economic, social, and ecological sustainability have finally found each other, as they should, but only at the ideological level.

The problem is, however, that this territorialist and historicist image goes against the real tendencies of contemporary urbanization, consisting of the development of technology and its spatial impacts, the specialization of expertise, and the growing power of the 'command and control' centres as the nodes of the network society. Even the growth of the elderly population does not necessarily imply the romantic vision of a contained community where people know and support each other. Nevertheless, the image prevails, and it is particularly strong in planning—understandably enough, since planning is still predominantly territorial, and people who escape from its view are considered a problem.

5 The politics of territorialism

In 1846, Pierre-Jean Proudhon published his reflections on political economy and socialism under the title *Philosophy of Poverty* (Philosophie de la misère). This inspired Karl Marx to write a critique of the book with the title *The Poverty of Philosophy* (La misère de la philosophie) in 1847. This play of words has lived on. The philosopher Karl Popper wrote in 1936 a paper called *The Poverty of Historicism*, published as an updated version in 1957, in which he developed a critique of teleological historicism. In his post-war publication *Open Society and its Enemies* from 1946, he traced the intellectual roots of historicism in Plato, Hegel, and Marx, among others. Finally, the planning theorist Andreas Faludi published in 2018 his book *The Poverty of Territorialism: A Neo-Medieval View of Europe and European Planning*. Actually, this was not just playing with words, since historicism and territorialism are connected in an interesting way.

As I argued in the previous chapters, conceptualizing either urbanity or urbanization with the concept of territory easily leads to confusions: an important feature of contemporary urbanization is that cities extend over their administrative borders, creating activities, infrastructure, and buildings within their region and between other city regions. There is no reasonable way to define where 'urban area' ends and where 'rural area' begins. Lefebvre went as far as suggesting to discard the concept of city altogether and start talking about urban society, complete urbanization, or planetary urbanization.

On the other hand, the administrative borders are still political borders, determining the legal rights of the city council and the rights of its formal citizens. One of these rights is the right to plan: to control land use and construction inside the perimeters of its sovereignty. If you cross the border, you are under the jurisdiction of another city or municipality. Regional authorities may have a right to prepare and approve regional plans for several municipalities, but even they have their external borders beyond which they have no authority. National governments, on the other hand, can determine the rules to be followed in planning—within their territory of sovereignty. Within their territory, cities, and municipalities usually commission experts to plan designated smaller areas for housing, industries, recreation, etc.

DOI: 10.4324/9781003124443-5

This hierarchical system of land use and construction would be logical if we were only planning the infrastructure and buildings within a designated area. Buildings, roads, ducts, and wires are physical things, and they are inherently local, fixed to the land that they occupy. The problems start if we imagine, either openly or tacitly, that we are planning for people. People are not fixed to the land that they occupy at any given moment: they are constantly on the move, and their movement easily crosses municipal, regional, and (during normal circumstances) even national borders, for instance within the Schengen-area. However, we tend to legitimize our plans by referring to what *people* need, what they prefer, or what is important to them. We may transcend their individual preferences by arguing that our solutions are sustainable in the long run, but even then, we tacitly refer to people: sustainability means satisfying *our* needs while preserving the possibility of *future generations* (of people) to satisfy *their* needs.

This inconsistency between the mobility of people and the territorial governance of local and national authorities is of course understandable from their different histories. The sovereignty of national governments and the imagined community and national identity that they are supposed to represent are defined by their borders and land, defended by military force. The people, in contrast, have for long been freed from their local dependence and extended their mobility networks using the development of the means of transport but also cultural and political change. They don't necessarily have strong local identities anymore, and many have no problems in identifying themselves with several localities or even globally. Networks and territories are, however, mutually inconsistent spatial entities. Since governance is meant to govern people, not only things, it needs to construct the imaginary 'people', 'citizens', or 'residents' who would stay within its territory of sovereignty. Such are naturally the state-men discussed earlier, but planning needs to go further in its imagination to ensure its legitimacy.

Here we come back to narratives that we started with. The local community, the urban village, the fifteen-minutes-city etc., are all narratives that interestingly go against the main trends of globalization, metropolization and the network society. We can watch Frank Capra's classical film *It's a Wonderful Life*, in which the main character is desperately trying to get out of his small town to the big world, but because of unexpected circumstances he needs to stay in his home town. In the end he understands that the local community that he has helped helps him in turn, making him 'the richest man in town'. As Alex Krieger writes in his book *City on a Hill* (Krieger, 2019), the small town has functioned as an important ideal in American urban development, echoing the moral superiority of permanent settlement against uprootedness, but also the territorialism that this implies.

It is interesting to notice that these Utopian urban narratives are mainly regressive: they do not describe elements of an imagined urban future where modern technologies, global connections, and metropolitan mentalities would form what Lefebvre called complete urbanization. Could such an imagined future community be an object of planning? At least not easily, since planning is dealing with land, and planning this land can only happen within a contained area of jurisdiction. Thus, as Faludi argues (Faludi, 2013; 2018), planning has tacitly adopted a 'container' view of territories, and that is something that he wants to reject. But are these two opposing spatial configurations compatible, and how?

We should study Faludi's argument more closely, but first I want to reflect on the historicist role of these regressive utopias. Popper's book Open Society and its Enemies was a polemical work against Plato, Hegel, and Marx, whose ideas lead, according to him, totalitarianism through their 'Utopian social engineering'. Instead, he suggested his own idea of 'piecemeal social engineering', a kind of incrementalism. This is something to which he gave less energy, but basically it means doing small social changes and assessing their successes or failures. It is reminiscent of his philosophy of science (Popper, 1975), in which hypotheses can be chosen freely but they have to be tested empirically. However, there is a lurking utopianism when this is applied in politics, since how can you assess your success without first having an idea of what kind of society you should strive for? Without going deeper into his arguments, however, it is interesting to consider two forms of Utopianism that he discusses, one going backwards in history (such as the Platonic), the other going forward to an imagined ideal state (such as the Marxist). Both can be found behind various planning ideologies.

Le Corbusier's ideology from the 1920s, for instance, can be said to represent Utopian social engineering; instead of incremental steps, he suggested even wiping historical cities to the ground to make way for his new shining cities, machines for living, working and working out (Le Corbusier, 1925). From the 60s onwards, as the modernistic planning ideas had materialized around the world, they also started raising critique that has continued to this day. Typically, the alternatives to his views have not been piecemeal social engineering but a wholesale discarding of modernist city planning and a return to at least the nineteenth century, if not to the medieval city. Thus, historicist thinking and planning is not historical, in the sense of basing its doctrines on an analysis of the contemporary situation in all of its details and its contextual potentialities, but rather on a 'paradise lost' or 'the city of future'. This legitimizing of today's planning and policies not on what *is* but on what *used to be* or what *will be*, is also the main target of the critique of idealistic planning and politics.

Let us consider two stories that represent the regressive utopias. In the early 1970s, a young planner Heikki Kaitera was commissioned to plan a new neighbourhood in Helsinki (Ryynänen, 2020). The big boom of modernistic suburban development was already waning, and planners were developing a renewed interest in more traditional urban development, including mixing of functions, ground floor shops and perimeter blocks. Kaitera was particularly critical of the CIAM principals of the separation of urban functions: apart from leading to more traffic, he saw that it produced an unpleasant environment, particularly for the pedestrians (Kaitera, 1982). He thought Camillo Sitte's praising of the medieval city again relevant, and from these ingredients he developed his doctrine of planning: mixing of housing and small industries in a neo-medieval setting, combined with very strict regulations. He was able to invite then famous architect Ralph Erskine to design some of the central buildings in the area. In short, his ideas represented pretty much what was later to be called New Urbanism.

The neighbourhood of Malminkartano was built according to the set regulations but, as might be expected, it did not become a medieval village. The small industries located among the housing blocks had nothing to do with the residents: providing jobs to the local people or selling products to them was not realistic in a small neighbourhood, and strict regulations only made it difficult for the businesses to grow and develop their activities. The residents also did not form a community, and the subsequent development of the neighbourhood has not been very successful: social problems and feelings of insecurity are much higher than on the average in Helsinki, and the city has included it in its special program of deprived neighbourhoods.

This New Urbanist ideology is also the governing principle of the much more recent comprehensive plan for the city of Helsinki, approved by the city council in 2016. One of the main ideas was to change all of the main arteries leading to the city into boulevards, thus freeing a substantial amount of space for housing and other urban functions. It also included extension of the densely built urban blocks in the city centre, as well as a network of rail tracks through sub-centres (making also them more compact). These were justified with the objective of creating an urban atmosphere (see the quotation in the introduction) but also agglomeration effects.

The strange thing in this rethinking of the urban structure was, however, that it was not based on a metropolitan or regional idea. The Helsinki metropolitan area consists of four cities: Helsinki, Espoo, Vantaa, and Kauniainen. Helsinki as the capital is of course largest with around 650 000 inhabitants, but the other two cities around it are not small either in the Finnish context, around 285 000 and 230 000, respectively, although Kauniainen is a small independent city of 9 500 inhabitants. In addition to the formal, registered citizens, however, Helsinki as the capital is used by many residents of the municipalities around the four cities, commuting to the city, as well as visitors and tourists. Naturally, the other metropolitan cities were worried about the potential weakening of the accessibility to the city centre of Helsinki. The state authority responsible for transportation and the environment also considered that access to the harbours and bus- and train stations was not guaranteed; the city had assumed that there would be road pricing to reduce the number of private cars, but such a decision had not been made, and it was not even under the jurisdiction of the city. The boulevards were also not included in the regional plan prepared and approved by the municipalities together. Consequently, the regional centre for employment, transportation and the environment (ELY) appealed to the Helsinki Administrative Court, and after the ruling of the Supreme Administrative Court, four of the suggested boulevards were considered illegal and had to be left out of the plan.

The common feature in both of these cases was that historicist territoriality was behind the imaginary of the planners of both Malminkartano and the city of Helsinki. As became clear in the Malminkartano case, people and businesses did not follow the imaginary urban village: the citizens who could choose were moving out as the social status of the neighbourhood weakened, which resulted in segregation. The businesses—if they stayed in the area—were hiring their workers from the catchment area of the whole metropolitan area, and they naturally sold their products to customers outside it—which is what businesses do in contemporary economies. Assessment of the results of the 2016 comprehensive plan in Helsinki is not yet available (the plan is targeted to the year 2050), but it is clear that the right to plan the area within the administrative borders (so-called 'planning monopoly') still dominates thinking of the planners and decision makers of the city. A corresponding return to the nineteenth century is not visible in the planning of the surrounding cities, and it was not supported by the state authorities.

Faludi's analysis of territorialism and its 'poverty' deals with the larger scale of the European Union. The EU is in principle a combination of sovereign member states. These have given part of their sovereignty to the union, but still the union is based on a voluntary contract between the member states. This became evident when the UK decided to leave the union and 'take back control': contracts can always be terminated, even if it can be expensive. The situation is totally different with regions seeking independence within states, such as Catalan in Spain or Scotland in the UK. National borders are specific; they are drawn in blood. The national governments are able to change the borders of their regions and municipalities by fiat, and they do that occasionally, but attempts to change their national borders means war; they are non-negotiable.

Faludi compares this with ownership: 'A land holding being a plot of land with its owner identified as such in some land registry means that it must be clearly marked; so there are walls, fences and the like surrounding plots—in other words physical barriers. At the very least, there are signs indicating where the border is, with appropriate warning like "No trespassing"' (Faludi, 2018, p. 26). While this may be true in Central Europe, it is not a universal feature of ownership: as already mentioned, in the Nordic countries where trekking, skiing or picking berries and mushrooms in forests has a long tradition, 'everyman's right' to these activities is protected by law, independently of the ownership of the land. Thus, potential fences or signs against trespassers are not legal borders, and anyone can cross these borders without breaking the law. This means, as Faludi also writes, (p. 43), that rights of property can only exist within a state which guarantees them, and which also determines what these rights include, for instance the right to develop one's land according to the requirements set by planning. This is something that local authorities cannot do, since the national state has the monopoly for legitimate use of force. Thus, territoriality of the European space is not a simple hierarchy: the jurisdictions of the subnational territories are delegated by the national state (and can be changed by it), but the EU, in contrast, is in a contractual relationship between the member states. They have delegated part of their sovereignty to the Union, but they have not 'surrendered' to it.

This reminds us of Foucault's famous reversal of Clausewitz's dictum that 'war is the continuation of politics by other means' (Foucault, 2004, p. 165). Since war is always present as a potential course of events, political decisions and regimes can only be understood as reflections of this background. Naturally, it is not a Hobbesian 'everybody's war against everybody' but a complicated web of existing and potential coalitions that can also be broken. If politics is, thus, 'continuation of war by other means', national citizenship remains as the key concept in spite of the European integration. Contractarian relationships are not inconsistent with sovereignty.

Nevertheless, the EU wants to promote what is called 'territorial cohesion': lagging regions should be strengthened and border areas used efficiently. This would require, according to Faludi, that we get rid of the understanding of member states as 'containers'. Container is a bit problematic metaphor, however, since what would it contain? Corporeal people and goods can freely move from one territory to another within the EU, and this is the very idea of the union. Land does not move, of course, and the EU does not have authority to plan the land-use of its member states. Instead of the 'hard' statutory planning, therefore, Faludi suggests that we should strive for a 'soft' planning that can avoid the 'Russian doll' understanding of the European space, where the scalar differences are seen as territories-within territories.

As Faludi pointed out already in 2013, (Faludi, 2013), there has been a certain optimism in planning literature about the potential permeability of the national borders and the corresponding new practices in planning. According to Rifkin, the EU is 'a first governing experiment in a world metamorphosing from geographic planes to planetary fields' (ref in Faludi, 2012). According to Clark and Jones, the EU is 'the only self-sustaining example of post-sovereign statehood.' (quotation in Faludi, 2012). However, this literature is mainly published before the pandemic or even before the refugee crisis of 2015, both of which strengthened the territoriality of the member states. They were serious blows to the idea of free mobility of people and things, which was behind the whole idea of integration. Under these 'special' circumstances, the member states adopted 'temporary' measures to control their borders, reducing the mobility of people to prevent unmanageable immigration or contagion, as well as reducing the free movement of their population inside their national borders. These measures were decided nationally, and they were based on the situation in different countries;

the governments naturally wanted to prevent, for instance, the virus entering from other countries with a worse situation. This was hardly 'soft' planning discussed by Faludi, even if it was not statutory. Many countries were caught by surprise, and it is evident that a more robust plan for such situations will be prepared for the future.

Is this spatial planning? In any case, it is spatial, and it has spatial effects to the economies of European regions—particularly the border regions that the EU has been interested in. The member states may be successful in their exit-strategies, but what will remain is an awareness of the risks. Thus, it also reminds us of the growing political risk of the refugee crisis exacerbated by the climate change. The borders have retained their political meaning, and there is no way that the EU could force them to open 'in times of crisis'.

In this sense, it is interesting to consider the alternatives of this traditional territorialism. What does it mean to say that 'any exclusive form of territoriality must be rejected' (Faludi, 2012)? We clearly have two senses of the word 'reject': academic rejection of a concept (because it does not adequately describe the political reality) and political rejection of it. Unlike in scientific discourses, political adopting and rejecting of concepts does not need to be consistent, but it is part of a political struggle, aiming at conceptual hegemony. Since EU is not a federal state, its legitimacy to influence land-use and economic activities within the territories of the member states is constantly negotiated, and not only that: political struggles within the member states keeps politicians alert in order to convince their citizens that essential national control is still maintained. Land is different from other policy areas, since it is historically the invasion or defence of the borders, i.e. territory, that defines the identity of nation states.

This identity is not so easily shattered. Faludi refers to Loriaux's interesting studies on the 'myths' on which the Rhineland frontier is based. According to him, it was Julius Caesar's invoking of artificial labels such as Gallia and Germania, 'marking the edge up to which it paid to keep Roman garrisons.' But even if this was a 'speech act', creating the subsequent (and still prevailing) national border between France and Germany, it is not only a myth: the keyword may indeed be the garrison. Thus, 'deconstructing' this frontier needs more than an act of will or a change of speech.

The problem is that territorial politics may be 'dormant' and reawaken if something unexpected happens. The fixed link between Malmö and Copenhagen had already created a twin city, but as the refugee crisis worsened and asylum seekers were searching their way through Denmark to Sweden, border control was 'temporarily' re-established. The ferries between Finland and Estonia and the EU-membership of the latter had also created a common border region, allowing Estonian workers to travel to Finland (where salaries were higher) for the week and return back home for the weekends. When the pandemic hit, border control and specific entry requirements were adopted, until commuting was made practically impossible. Retirees living in Spain and Finland, on the other hand, were stuck in unilocality, as flights were cancelled and entering to most countries inside and outside the EU was heavily restricted. Even if economic development and the mobility of people had made it possible to develop strategic or 'soft' planning and policies, with permeable borders, this did not last when the times became hard. Literature on planning in the integrated Europe has often sounded unprecise and complicated, and this may indeed reflect the actual situation where traditional national power and contractual integration have met each other. In the end, however, it is power that matters. In spite of contrary aspirations, this is also where Faludi's arguments lead us:

> Realism demands, though, that the limits of what is possible are taken into account. Hard spaces are entrenched because they are the bases for the organisation in wards, constituencies, electoral districts, and so forth, of democratic decision making. For as long as there are no convincing alternatives to this manner of producing legitimacy, hard spaces will remain the primary building blocks for territorial organisation.
>
> (ibid., p. 1313)

Where does this leave us, in terms of multi-locality? The European space with permeable borders and soft planning is clearly the space of corporeal people and material things. Their movement is what produces the 'Neo-Medieval' Europe that Faludi (referring to Zielonka) is suggesting, as a replacement of 'Westphalian' territorialism, so called after the Peace of Westphalia of 1648 (Faludi, 2018, p. 64). This agreement included the recognition of the right of sovereigns to govern their territories and peoples, which is still behind the contemporary territorialism in Europe, although this 'recognition' has been broken in several wars in which the sovereigns have tried to redraw their borders.

What Faludi and Zielonka are after is a European spatial governance and planning that would somehow be based on the movements, networks, and functional organizations that form the 'reality' of the spatial organization of Europe. Zielonka mentions transport, energy, migration, tourism and sport as examples as such 'overlapping jurisdictions'. According to Faludi, 'national sovereignty is meaningful only where national borders coincide with market transaction fringes, military frontiers and migration trails. In terms of the analogy with animal behaviour [...] it would make sense only where the home range of people coincides with the national territory, which is not the case—at least not for everybody' (Faludi, 2018, p. 116).

One may ask, however, what this 'making sense' would mean in the context of the politics of territoriality. Transport, migration, tourism and sports were the activities and industries that were most severely damaged when the pandemic closed borders and postponed events, such as the Olympic Games in Tokyo. The EU could help the member states financially, but closing and opening the borders were under the jurisdiction of the member states themselves. One may also ask whether the analogy from animal behaviour is to the point. States have never been the natural home ranges of people; they have always been based on interaction like trade in addition to exclusion of competitors. So, Faludi is right: national territories as containers don't make sense, but there they are. Even if national borders would seem to be softening or even disappearing when the weather is good, they are easily reintroduced in times of crisis. Hard times call for hard measures, and people will again be categorized as insiders or outsiders, even within the EU.

Thus, it seems to me that there is and always has been an inconsistency between the networks of people's activities and the territoriality of governance and planning. As the two planning cases in Helsinki demonstrate, this can lead to spatial imaginaries that try to reconstruct a new territoriality reminiscent of historical models, such as the medieval or the nineteenth century city. Naturally enough, their proponents don't see themselves as regressive but rather brave and innovative; historicism can look at both directions in its critique of the state of the art.

Should Faludi's Neo-Medieval view of spatial planning, then, belong to the same category of historicism? This depends on its ability to connect its analysis and planning practice to the existing and emergent power relationships and production. As Faludi rightly points out, territorialism is not God's will or in our genes but rather a social and political construction. As such, however, it can only be demolished by a counteracting power. The functional networks of individuals, organizations and corporations are using the degrees of freedom given to them to pursue their interests, adapting themselves to both the national and the EU regulations. But can planning follow these activities and networks? As I have argued, states with their statistics are not able or even willing to follow them, being content with satisfying the imagined needs of the state-men that define both their jurisdiction and their obligations.

In structural terms, the Neo-Medieval Europe is of course the opposite of territorialism defined by the jurisdiction of planning. If a planner is given the task to plan a neighbourhood—and only that, since there are other planners responsible for planning the other side of the border—he may construct an imaginary community with jobs, shops, and people staying in the area. If he is given the task of planning a whole city, even this can be seen a larger territory, forming the 'Russian doll' spatiality that Faludi is opposing. But what would be an alternative practice that would avoid such territorialism? Unfortunately, this alternative is something that he is unable to describe: 'I am often asked for an alternative. No, I have no blueprint.' (ibid., p. 150). The problem seems to be that territorialism—although by no means natural or ahistorical—is born out of power, and it can only be deconstructed by power. It may indeed be that planning as part of the state apparatus is not the way to transgress boundaries, no matter how rational it would be. Luckily, people themselves have much better opportunities to do it.

6 Political topology

Multi-locality as a concept is often restricted to some of its sub-categories, such as residential multi-locality in two or more homes. This leads to the understanding of the phenomenon as a special case, concerning only a small elite of those who are willing and able to invest in several houses or apartments, or at least the middle classes who have for long used second homes during their weekends and holidays. In order to avoid this, we should perhaps start our discussion on 'political topology' with the most precarious multi-locals, the homeless.

This may sound strange at first. How can you reside in *many* places if you don't have *any* place to stay? This may again be related to the general confusion of the corporeal and the state-persons. Losing one's home does not mean ceasing to exist as a corporeal human being, it only means that the normative pair 'person-address' ceases to exist. Since (corporeal) persons and addresses belong to different ontological categories, their combination is neither a body nor a geographical location. 'Usually, what is counted in the census are not simply "the people", bodies, individuals or citizens, but rather people-in-homes-with-addresses' writes Nadine Marquardt (Marquardt, 2016). This calls for some reflection. What could we mean by 'people-in-homes-with-addresses', as people are mostly not at home? This is, it seems, an administrative construction, since even in the 'normal' case—when people are not homeless—the location of the body and the address are not tied to each other. Only the state-person and the address, as constructions by the state with statistics, belong to the same ontological category, in the sense that neither are material.

But what does happen when people become homeless? If the formal addresses are missing, they in a way escape from the view of the state, they become 'non-existent'. As corporeal human beings, however, they need to occupy several places: streets and courtyards, shelters, stations, parks, etc. The difference from living (partly) in one 'legitimate' home is, first of all, that these places can be occupied only temporarily, and there is no sovereignty over them. Public places such as parks and stations are easier to use, since in private spaces residents and security quickly intervene. Second, the functions that are usually performed centrally at home (sleeping, cooking,

DOI: 10.4324/9781003124443-6

eating, washing, using toilets) need to be distributed to different places. Often this means that public and private spaces are mingled or superimposed. This is an extreme form of forced multi-locality, but ontologically it is not so different from counting 'normal' people who are not corporeally occupying the address that they are connected to. The difference is the political status of the formal address: many of the social services (even if they are serving the body) are tied to the address: the municipality in which the address is entitled to provide the services, but only within its territory. The political rights are also partly address-based; even if you don't lose your citizenship when you lose your home, homelessness is a negation, not-being somewhere.

This negative ontology of the homeless is interesting, as it seems to be complete: there are no concepts that could positively characterize the homeless. Non-urban, for instance, can be classified as suburban, exurban or rural, giving these areas (and the corresponding cultures and ways of life) positive characteristics, even if they are abstracted and do not correspond to the corporeal activities and mobility of the people themselves. Suburban people don't stay in the suburbs, and they all have unique characteristics, but we call them suburban, since their formal address is in a suburb. If we study multi-locality of 'normal' people having an address, we may use official statistics to determine their 'homes' or 'domiciles' and use this as one of the places that multi-local people use.

But the situation becomes more difficult if we study the homeless people. First of all, we cannot send them letters inviting them to participate in a survey. They cannot be represented in a random sample provided by statistics institutes. They lack the key location used in most studies of the use of urban space, the home. Homes are particular in the sense that the dwellers have sovereignty over them, either by themselves or negotiated with their partners or family members. This is usually guaranteed by the state through legislation. The homeless, on the other hand, have a number of activity places where they sleep, eat, work or spend time, without having sovereignty over any of them. Their precariousness is, thus, also spatial, not only economic, although these are clearly connected: you need to be able to shower and wash your clothes to apply or keep your job (Huffman et al., 2021). Without a *domus*, you cannot *dominate* any part of the urban space.

This ontological negativity could perhaps be countered by counting, but this is also challenging without the address. One can try to explain the reasons for homelessness by counting their previous addresses (as Culhane et al. 1996 have done, ref. Iwata & Karato, 2011). They found out, unsurprisingly, that homeless families come from areas with a high proportion of boarded-up housing and persons living below the poverty line. This is of course dependent on the country and their welfare and social housing systems. However, this kind of counting is still negative, since the people are not living there anymore; the way that the homeless people are living and where can only be known by counting them as corporeal human beings. They—if anyone—are living as bodies, exposed to the cold, rain, and wind.

Counting bodies is, however, a double-edged sword. It may be a way to make them *count*, as Marquardt (2016) aptly puts it, but it is also exposing them under surveillance. Modern technology with face-recognition can be used to follow each person individually, whether they are homeless or not, but in democratic societies this is considered a violation of their privacy. Nevertheless, homeless people can be guaranteed individual rights only by recognizing them individually. For some this is not a problem, but if you are, for instance, both homeless and paperless, you would like to avoid such individuation. '– – rough sleepers, and especially women and migrants, have many reasons to try staying invisible, as they are in high risk of being (sexually) harassed or ticketed for illegal camping. Therefore, they are notoriously difficult to count' (ibid.).

The alternative is to count the number of homeless in different places, in order to see what features of these places are relevant to the homeless as a group. This is what Iwata and Karato did, by using already existing data from homeless count from 1998, consisting of the number of homeless spending time in different census blocks of Osaka City. They found out that, in addition to the homeless networks, they were concentrated in the *Kamasagi yoseba* or business districts where employment opportunities are offered. 'These findings suggest that Japanese homeless people have a strong will to work. In Japan, homeless people begging in the street are very rare'. This clearly indicates that they are 'deserving poor'. In contrast, Nadine Marquardt discusses the German national government's *refusal* to establish a homeless statistics, as part of 'ontological ignorance'. '[T]he national government again argues that there is no need for a homeless statistic, because homelessness today is no longer caused by a lack of housing, but by a range of other socio-psychological problems'.

It seems that homelessness is a form of multi-locality where the supreme morality of the place and 'rootedness' as against constant mobility and vagabondage create a specific precariousness. The ontology of negativity— the fact that none of the activity places of homeless people determine their existence—also allows the absurd policies that some municipalities have adopted to 'cleanse' the city centres from visible homeless. When choosing places by themselves, the homeless people tend to prefer public and central places, for several reasons: they are not so easily harassed, they can find things that they need for survival, such as remains of food or empty bottles, or they can find sheltered places to sleep or available toilets. For the city authorities developing their images as successful and vibrant cities, these visible and active homeless are seen as a problem, and hard measures to restrict their presence and their only remaining ways to survive, are taken to use (Petty & Young, 2020).

It is understandable, though, that the spatiality of the homeless is not usually interpreted as multi-locality, since we are still tied to the primacy of place over movement and the supposed inconsistency in being in a place and being on the go. Homelessness is also something that most of us have never experienced, and, if our city management is successful in 'cleansing' the centre, do not even see and, thus, can imagine away. This can be done by providing shelters far from the centre or, more humanely, housing in less favourable neighbourhoods that we have no reason to visit.

It is strange, however, that one of the most common forms of multi-locality, commuting, is not usually recognized as such, even though there are, by definition, at least two places involved. Commuting is of course the natural effect of urban growth, as the concentration of jobs in cities does not correspond to the availability of affordable housing in them, or the availability of qualities preferred by people (such as one-family houses or natural environments) close to where the jobs are.

The concept of affordability is not as easily defined as one might expect, and sometimes it is even confused with low rents and prices of apartments. The second necessary condition is, of course, that the living costs match the disposable income of potential residents—generally 30 percent of the disposable income is considered a reasonable share. It is most often connected to low-income residents, but in principle these conditions have to be met by all residents of the city: you need to afford your living arrangements, whether it is by renting or owning—one or several homes.

However, this is not enough, since the housing arrangements should naturally be connected with the urban structure of cities. You can always find an affordable home in a place where there are no jobs or services. Instead, you need to find a home within a reasonable distance from the workplace where you need to work daily, or at least show up. You also need basic services, such as nurseries, schools, or health care centres, again within a reasonable distance—but from what? This is the key conceptual problem of commuting, if we follow the 'taken-for-granted' way of thinking. You need to reach the services, but it is not self-evident that the ideal location for them is close to your formal address. Commuters usually have their formal addresses in other municipalities, and these municipalities are expected to provide them with the municipal services—within a reasonable distance from their formal address. However, if the citizens are working in the city, it might make more sense if they could, for instance, fetch their children from the nursery or see a doctor closer to their workplace. Again, it seems that planning of municipal services and the corresponding planning of land-use and construction are not directed to the human beings but to the municipality itself. The commuters are working in the city, but they are not citizens of the city.

The traditional practice of commuting can be seen as an offspring of the basic rhythm of the industrial city—or remnants of it. In pre-industrial societies, activities had to be coordinated, but not according to the clock. Farmers were following the natural rhythms of the day and the year, shopkeepers had to synchronize their presence with their customers, and craftsmen had to organize their work according to their commissioners and workforce. Industrialization changed this, since the workers had to be present at an exact time, together with their fellow workers, to work with the machinery. Their presence became necessary: if they were absent for some reason, they had to be replaced to allow others to work. If their absence could be tolerated for a while in certain jobs (e.g. cleaning), it could be used as an incentive: if others had to do your work while you were away, this created a social pressure to avoid unnecessary absences. This system created the basic rhythm of the industrial city and its peak hours, with employees going to work in the morning at the same time and leaving again in the afternoon. The rest is history: the density of the cities and the poor housing conditions, the emergence of public transportation to allow expansion of the city, the dominance of the private car, the huge investments in transportation infrastructure, suburban development, urban sprawl, and commuting.

As industrial work in the factory was more and more replaced by white-collar work in the offices, the latter were still following the logic of the factory: the employees were expected to arrive at the same time, their working was managed within the office by representatives of the employer, they were sitting by their desks in pretty much the same way as factory workers by their machines. Working time and workplace were tightly connected: the employees were selling their working hours to the employer, the salaries were based on this time (not, for instance, on the results), the employees needed a permission to leave the workplace, etc. (Gajendran & Harrison, 2007). As the labour unions became stronger and the welfare state developed, they targeted their activities and pressure to the same elements: raising salaries (by the hour), protecting the employees from exploitation by determining the maximum working hours, and guaranteeing insurance at the workplace or on the way to it. This has led to absurdities as work and workplace are losing their tight connection. For instance, employees doing work at home may be insured while sitting at their desks but not when they go to the toilet.

I shall return to the logic of presence and absence in the next chapter, but let us first continue with the commuters. The industrial-office work set the stage for commuting: even if insured, commuters usually do not get paid for the time they spend in travelling to the workplace, even if they are required to be there on time. If the 'disposable time' of the day is divided roughly into three—eight hours of work, eight hours of sleep, and eight hours of free time—the time for travelling is taken from the free time, which means that it is actually not free. As the commuting times tend to grow, the result is 'métro, boulot, dodo', as the French say: most of the daily time goes to getting to the workplace, working, returning to home, doing some necessary activities like eating, and sleeping. Even though the working hours have been reduced in the work contracts, commuting times have become longer because of the lack of affordable housing closer to the workplaces.

Commuters themselves must have felt frustrated for travelling an hour or so to the office to do the work that they could as well have done at home, or in another place closer to home. It has not been like this for long, though. Even if office workers have mainly been handling information for decades, they have until recently been dependent on the information stored in files and folders at the office—physical files and folders or information that could only be accessed within the office. The computers at the office have also been much better than their home computers, if they even had one. Computer networks were not fast enough to handle big files. They also needed to meet their colleagues and customers face-to-face.

All this has now changed, and they are able to 'telecommute'. This word is reminiscent of the early word 'horseless carriage', since if you can telework from home or from other more convenient locations, such as coffee shops, libraries, or co-working spaces, you are not 'commuting' to the office and back again. But the other available terms are problematic as well. Probably the most commonly used term is remote work, but it implicitly assumes that there is one location from which the working is 'remote'. The work arrangements including the office and the home are still the most common, but as the hybrid working arrangements and the role of the main office are rapidly changing, you may already ask: remote from what? If you are able to work with your laptop at home but also in libraries, cafés and public transport, can your work be any closer? The terms telework and multi-local work that I have chosen to use in this book do not carry such connotations of remoteness or commuting, while they also emphasize the role of technology (unlike the preindustrial handicraft that was also made at home).

Allen et al. (2015) made a review of the different concepts used for telecommuting and related activities, such as distributed work, flexible work arrangements, remote work, telework, and virtual teams. They concluded that the word telecommuting should only be used if the employee is hired in a large organization, is working only partly out of the main office, and is working mainly at home. This definition is fair, if we want to keep the term telecommuting as close as possible to physical commuting. However, if we consider this phenomenon from the employer's perspective, it is not important if employees are working at home or somewhere else—in any case they have 'escaped' the physical surveillance of the management. It is of course natural that teleworkers are mostly using their homes: they are already paid for, they are often empty during the day, one has the natural sovereignty of one's home, and the dress can be casual, unless one needs to perform in a teleconference. But they can also choose other places for working, the main point being that they *are chosen*. This major spatial change in the freedom and independence of the employee is why I consider it more appropriate to use the more general term *telework*.

Even before the pandemic, employers recognized that teleworking is a way to reduce real estate costs or paying high rents for office space that was only partly used. During the pandemic, this situation became even more pronounced, as the offices stood almost empty while most of the employees were sent home to telework. At the time of writing, the firms are preparing for the post-pandemic era, and this will most probably mean hybrid work arrangements, as most of the employees are willing to continue teleworking for at least part of the week. This gives the opportunity to rethink the 'main office', getting rid of its industrial pedigree. The employers could, for instance, mimic the places that employees have freely chosen if allowed to, such as cafeterias and libraries that we have studied as new working spaces (Di Marino & Lapintie, 2015; 2017). They may also redefine the office into a meeting place instead of a space where people sit and work throughout the day.

When a substantial number of people are working multi-locally, the whole concept of work has to change. It will take some time, since the industrial heritage of our working culture is so strong. When working time used to coincide with the workplace, then logically the time spent outside the workplace could not be work, unless it was a specific business trip, with a permission and strict rules on how to travel, how much time to spend, etc. If working time cannot be measured with presence, how can it be measured? Or should it? On the other hand, if it is not measured, how is it compensated? By results? But are we talking about the quantity or quality of the results? Freelance journalists have been paid by the centimetres they have written, and salesmen have been paid by the items they have sold. Most of us, however, are selling our time to our employers. We may get bonuses and eventually pay rise if we succeed in our work, but time is still the main measure of our input.

In multi-local teleworking, the managers have to develop new types of leadership. One manager we met told us a story of his employee who was allowed to telework a couple of days in a week. When he needed to talk to him, he called him on Friday afternoon and could hear that he was in a car, with children keeping noise at the back seat. He was probably going to his summer cottage, the manager thought, even though he should have been teleworking. Working time is still there in the background, even though it cannot be measured by presence. There is evidently a fear of losing control. 'The unpredictability of some of the work causes particular concern. For example, how would a manager know whether the worker had really encountered a problem that took longer to resolve than expected or whether the worker was slacking off?' (Koroma et al., 2014).

Employees may also misinterpret the idea of telework. Another manager told in the media that her employees might ask, for instance, whether they could telework next day, since they had already worked so many hours during the week. In other words, they confused teleworking with free time. Other employees would say that they didn't feel well, and asked if they could telework instead of coming to the office. That is, they confused teleworking with sick leave. This manager had another strategy: she allowed teleworking, but only in the middle of the week, thus preventing the potential extended weekends. Even in this case, she was managing time, not results.

A third manager of a big IT company told us that their employees were allowed to telework (actually using and thus experimenting with the software that they were selling), but they should be reachable at any time. He even refused to use the common term 'remote work', calling it 'presence work' instead—meaning *virtual* presence. He demonstrated this practice by contacting one of his employees, unannounced. She answered but told him that she had just come out of shower. 'OK, let's not put the cameras on', the manager said. This was also managing the working time. In the office, managers can drop in at any time to the rooms or by the desks of their employees, 'managing by walking around', as yet another manager called it. They cannot drop into the homes of their employees unannounced, but they can keep them alert by the *possibility* of calling them during the 'office hours'. Even though this is not surveillance, it could still be called a sort of Panopticism. These techniques, however, reduce one of the most important positive impacts of teleworking found in literature, the increased self-control of the employee (Gajendran & Harrison, 2007; Magnavita et al., 2021).

Conceptualizing telework as multi-local work instead of only working at home makes sense, since we don't need to make unjustified theoretical distinctions between those who are using their homes and those who choose another location (or between the times they are using them). The problem for research is, of course, that it is difficult if not impossible to follow the corporeal people changing their workplaces several times a day. This is why researchers would like to choose questions that can be answered using statistics, such as the home addresses and the locations of the main offices. The danger is, however, that one ends up following the state-people, not the corporeal people. It is also common that the industrial city keeps looming in the background with its daily, weekly, and yearly rhythms.

One possibility is to try to catch people 'in the act' and interview them. This will not allow statistical (sic) generalizations, but it can reveal some of the ways that mobile workers use in their orientation in urban space. We used this approach by searching people in potential spaces that could be used for working outside the office and home, such as coffee shops and libraries, and asked them to participate in our research project (Di Marino & Lapintie, 2015; 2017). We found several reasons for choosing these non-traditional workplaces. Scholars but also entrepreneurs of start-ups were using libraries as informal offices, since they were free, calm and provided wi-fi-networks and printing facilities. Some would use both libraries and cafeterias on their way to meet their customers. Some others wanted to escape from the office to a café in order to concentrate without constant social interaction with their colleagues. Some would mention several of these reasons, which indicates that 'ideal types' are not capturing the reality of their itineraries—even if they can be used to develop multifunctional spaces.

Such spaces can be used for working, even if their primary function would be something else. Consider, for instance, spaces that are called 'waiting rooms' and are designed for waiting, usually provided with sofas, armchairs, coffee tables, and old magazines. However, there is hardly any function that is more absurd than 'waiting'? One might, for instance, want to read one's e-mail, glance a text that is being prepared, prepare a presentation, etc., *while waiting*. Facilities for this purpose are for instance desks, ergonomic chairs, power outlets, and wi-fi connections.

Unlike advertised by some mobile phone companies and service providers, people are not working in any place whatsoever, even if the technology would allow this. Places do not disappear along with IT, but, to the contrary, people are comparing them with each other based on their characteristics. Multi-locality opens the potentialities for locational choice, and in that sense, it is an empowering phenomenon. On the other hand, it is a challenging working practice: Koroma et al. (2014) analyse the several hindrances that mobile workers face when they try to find suitable working conditions in places that are not always designed for work. The freedom to choose is of course dependent on the type of work and work arrangements, but it challenges the sedentary lifestyle that is still often taken for granted.

Let us consider a case of a man who was a retired civil engineer but still wanted to do some work every now and then. He was living in the city but was offered work opportunities in another region, 400 kilometres away, too far to commute. Although most of the work could be done remotely, he still needed to participate in meetings and public hearings. What to do? Instead of renting a work apartment or staying in a hotel and driving five hours for a meeting, he decided to buy a recreational vehicle. In this way, he could combine a personal office, a home, and recreational activities. After a meeting he could simply go home—to his second home parked nearby. When he needed to work, he simply turned his driving seat around, and there he was, by his desk, using his laptop and mobile connections. He could choose a nice location by the sea, open the doors and enjoy, instead of sitting in a small office in the city. When he had free time, he could simply take the vehicle to the use it was originally built for, recreation.

Although this is not a lifestyle for everyone, it again shows how difficult it is to use our traditional concept like home, workplace, office, summer cottage, or private car in a spatial context where all these are superimposed. Mobile instead of sedentary lifestyle is the keyword. It also shows how challenging multi-locality can be for research. Is this telecommuting? According to Allen et al. (2015) it is, but it is hardly something that they had in mind. Is it living? Surely it is for the corporeal man, even though the state-man remains tightly in his apartment in the city where he is registered. It seems that nothing is gained by trying to force 'new wine into old bottles', i.e. the emerging phenomenon of multi-locality into the conceptual framework tacitly based on unilocality.

7 The logic of presence and absence

> [...] Pierre's absence from the café doesn't *mean* the same as his presence at home (although the latter entails the former—which is equally entailed by his death) any more than it means the same as Jean's occupying his customary place.
>
> (Bhaskar, 1993, p. 7)

This quotation from Roy Bhaskar's *Dialectic; The Pulse of Freedom* exemplifies his logic of absence, which is a complicated theory but—as this example, referring to Sartre, demonstrates—still intuitive. We only need to add a third place where Pierre could have been present or absent, the office, and we have the whole problematic of multi-locality, with its integration of work and residing. Though intuitive, this example opens the way to another difficulty of empirical research on multi-locality, comparable to what I was discussing in Chapter 3 on modalities. Modalities (e.g. what can happen, what can be known, believed or perceived, or what should not be done) are problematic because they are real, not imagined or subjective, but they cannot be directly perceived. But modal logic is not the same as the logic of absence.

Consider the possible methods that we can use—and have used—to study empirically how people are really living their lives in a multi-local setting. Ourselves, we used observation to find the people who were working in unusual places. We also used qualitative interviews to learn why and where they had been earlier, and where they used to work (Di Marino & Lapintie, 2015; 2017). Our colleagues at Aalto University studied quantitatively the places that people used in their everyday life 'during a normal week' (Hasanzadeh et al., 2021). They used the official statistics of the primary residence and the everyday activity points of a sample of 10 000, using a combination of interactive maps and surveys.

We could also study their mobility with diaries, or their use of time in different places. We could even use mobile phone data to see where people were concentrated at certain times of the day or week. We could also study their use of second homes and how much time they used for different

DOI: 10.4324/9781003124443-7

activities there. But what is absent? Absence. In the same way as empirical research is usually tacitly committed to *actualism*, it is also committed to *positivism*, or 'ontological monovalence' as Bhaskar calls it. According to this doctrine, only things that *are* there, in spatio-temporal relationships with each other (when and where), and the events they perform, are *real*. But this would mean that Pierre's absence from the café would *not* be real, even though it cannot be translated into positive events, like his being at home.

If we change this to a case of teleworking, we cannot deny that Pierre is absent from the office while he is teleworking. This absence is, however, not the same thing as his working at home, or in a library, or in a café. Somebody may also be sitting by Pierre's desk, but he is still absent. Thus, it is possible for Pierre to be absent and present at the same time, and both of these facts have real consequences. Absences can be real (real negations), and they can be causally responsible for certain effects.

Let us consider that you should be at the office at 8 am, but you are 15 minutes late. Your manager notices this, and when you arrive, he may say 'you are late' (as if you wouldn't know that) or 'where have you been?' (as if your location 15 minutes ago would be relevant). What is relevant is that your absence was illegitimate, and you could be criticized for it. The critique was not directed at your work or your results; if you had been on time, nobody would have required you to demonstrate results within the first 15 minutes. Having been criticized, you can offer excuses (I was caught in a traffic jam, I missed the bus, my car didn't start, etc.). You would not say, for instance, that 'I had a great idea, and I had to sit down for a while to think about it'. This is because you were not criticized for your poor performance but only for your absence. Traditional office work is indeed following the logic of the factory: even if there wouldn't be any reason for simultaneity or contiguity of the workers, these requirements have still remained in many organizations. Thus, we could say that it has not actually been *time* that we have been selling to our employers, but our *presence*. One traditional manager even said that those who arrive late or leave early (than they should) are 'stealing from their employer'.

Absence (as a sort of 'nothingness') is ontologically interesting. In the example that Bhaskar is referring to, Sartre is himself 15 minutes late from his appointment with Pierre and, knowing that Pierre is usually very punctual, wants to know whether he is still there or whether he has left (Sartre, 1992, p. 40). It seems that Pierre is not there any longer, he is absent. What does this observation mean? Clearly, the café is full of presences, positivities (other customers, waiters, bar counter, coffee machines, etc.), but Sartre is not interested in them, they in a way retreat to the background, on top of which Sartre is looking for Pierre. But since Pierre is not there, his *absence* is revealed on top of this background. And nothing in the background entails his absence.

Your manager can also try to find you in the office, but the plenitude of positivities that he can see (other workers, your empty desk, the fact that others have not seen you) are not enough to entail your absence, although these will be observed by him. You are 'out of sight', out of his control, but also out of the positive support (information, feeling of importance) that you could give him. Conversely, the absence of a manager will leave the workers alone when they would need support or guidance. 'My door is always open', one Chief Executive told his employees to highlight his support for them. 'What does it help if the door is open if there is nobody there', one of his employees commented later (after leaving his job, naturally). Absence is a real negation, and it should be treated as such. The CE naturally was somewhere, in business trips, in board meetings, in negotiations, in meetings with shareholders, etc., but, as Bhaskar remarked, these do not *mean* the same as his being absent from his office.

Naturally, the paradox of the office-as-factory has been understood for a long time, but the cultural difficulties could explain the slow development into more reasonable working arrangements. People have been offered flexibility in their working hours: they have been allowed to arrive later if they also leave later, or if their working hours are balanced within a certain period. Nevertheless, the change is dramatic if and when working changes into a hybrid mode or complete teleworking. Does it mean that some people are *never* present and *always* absent? If one cannot avoid being absent by being present somewhere else, the real effects of this absence need to be taken into account.

The simultaneity of presence and absence has, however, always been part of the traditional work-life experience. When you are present at the office, you are at the same time absent from home. If you are working long hours, you have less time to spend with your partner and play with your children. Poor work-life balance may lead to estrangement and even divorce. Being present and absent have different emotional characteristics. As Bhaskar mentioned, absence can also be the result of one's death. Theoretical absences or absences of unknown people do not have the same force: we may miss only people we have known, and this absence can remain for the rest of our lives (e.g. the death of a husband or wife, the death of a child). On the other hand, the situation may also be reversed: one may be glad of another's absence and fear for his presence, as in violent relationships.

The major change in this traditional setting is the possibility of virtual presence and absence. One may be present in a meeting with people who are also virtually present or in the office. One may be present in social media or chat. On the other hand, one may be absent in the physical space by distancing oneself from the surroundings. As mobile smartphones have become our necessary extensions, they have also created a kind of 'absent-mindedness', alternating between virtual and corporeal presence, being here and not here. Multi-tasking is not possible for human beings, only continuous shifting from absences to presences, and back again.

The major risk that teleworkers face if they are very seldom present is that they are not equally recognized in the community, their commitment may be in doubt, and chances of promotion weakened. Physical presence is still an important element to create and maintain trust. On the other hand, the ability to concentrate and the time saved from travelling may lead to increased productivity that rational leadership should recognize.

The fear of the employees and the prejudice of the managers are actually not very well grounded in research results. There is already a lot of studies on the impacts of allowing employees to adopt different types of teleworking. In their extensive review of this literature, Allen et al. (2015) note, for instance, that teleworking has been positively associated with job satisfaction, commitment to the organization, as well as supervisor-rated and objectively measured job performance. '[…] firms with larger proportion of telecommuters also exhibited the greatest innovation and financial and relational performance (e.g. product and process innovation and labor, customer, and supplier relations)' (ibid., p. 50). As the unfounded prejudices have probably diminished during the pandemic, it is evident that teleworking will remain as part of the working arrangements that rational employers adopt in the future.

Among the positive impacts of teleworking discussed by Allen et al. (2015) there is, however, one item that is crucial for our purposes. Referring to Dionne and Dostie (2007) and Stavrou (2005), they conclude that 'telecommuting relates to reduced absenteeism even when controlling for several firm characteristics'. Indeed, Dionne and Dostie argue that 'Using detailed data on the scheduling of the work week, we find that workers who worked at home or worked on a reduced work week had a lower incidence of absenteeism[…]' (Dionne & Dostie, 2007).

But how can one be absent while working at home? As mentioned, employees are always absent from their workplaces when they are teleworking. Absenteeism, on the other hand, is conceptually derived from the industrial tradition of work, according to which workers produce value to employers only when they are present at the 'workplace'. Being absent means a loss, whether it is for a reason (such as illness) or illegitimate. As economists, Dionne and Dostie assume absenteeism to be a rational choice of the *homo economicus*: 'When a worker contracts for more than his desired hours given w [wage rate], he retains an incentive to consume more leisure. One way of doing so is to be absent from work' (ibid, p. 109). Other scholars would be interested in such issues as ethical commitment, social attachment to co-workers, pride in one's work or identification as a skilled worker or leading professional. The interesting question here is, however, that the whole concept of absenteeism seems to be completely outdated.

If Pierre is working at home, does his being absent mean that he is also absent from home? Perhaps he is in a café instead, meeting Sartre? But if he is a philosopher or a publisher, for instance, his encounter with Sartre could be part of his job. But as we remember, he is also absent from the café when Sartre arrives 15 minutes late (at the time of the writing of *Being and Nothingness* in 1943, there were no mobile phones, so he could assume that

Sartre would not come). Is this an act of absenteeism? But what if he went to the library to continue his work after missing his encounter with Sartre? In addition to this positivity, there is of course a multitude of absences, and even counting them all will not justify us to say that his action is an instance of absenteeism. Positivity is 'a tiny, but important, ripple on the surface of a sea of negativity', as Bhaskar puts it. Just like 'working time', presence at the 'workplace' is no longer an adequate measure of work if the worker is allowed to work somewhere else, which does not have to be his home.

Considering this absurdity of defining work with either time or presence, we may even need a new theory of work. Such an endeavour is outside the scope of this book, but perhaps it makes sense to ask why the concept of work is so often conflated with presence. For instance, the literature on absenteeism usually takes it for granted that illegitimate absence is a problem for the employer, representing an additional cost that needs to be diminished by various means, such as surveillance and penalties. On the other hand, as Ruhle and Süß (2019) argue, the opposite of absenteeism, 'presenteeism' can be equally problematic if employees report at the workplace even when they are sick. This may lead to productivity loss and even increased subsequent absences if the disease is contagious—something that was highlighted during the pandemic, as workers were asked to stay home even with mild symptoms of flu.

What, in the end, is the problem with absenteeism? It is clear that industrial production requires synchronization of workers' attendance and activities, and even pre-industrial work before clock-time needed coordination and the corresponding discipline. Nevertheless, the objective of work is clearly that things get done: products are produced, buildings are built and music composed. Spending time at the workplace and attending meetings are not objectives as such, they can only be justified if they are necessary or at least useful for the main objective of work. One can spend time at the workplace without getting anything done (and still receive the salary based on 'working hours'), and attending many meetings can be highly unproductive. On the other hand, absence from the 'workplace', such as an office, can be highly productive.

Consider the different reasons that people give for using non-traditional workplaces such as cafés and libraries (Di Marino & Lapintie, 2015). One may, for instance, need to 'leave work to get work done': the main office may contain so many distractions that it is difficult to do tasks that require concentration. Paradoxically, a crowded café may be a more suitable place for it, even if there is noise of coffee machines and people coming and going. The Simmelian 'metropolitan mentality' allows us to move all this to the background, since there are no social obligations, unlike in the office. This kind of absence (from the office) clearly *increases* the productivity of the employee. If the management would require everybody to work inside the office, this would actually be counterproductive to the employer.

The second type of multi-local workers we found were mobile workers who had several meetings with customers in different places. If they had a couple of hours between meetings, it made no sense to return to the main office and back again. Instead, they searched for places like cafés or libraries to read their e-mails or prepare their presentations. This is not easy, since cities are not yet designed as multifunctional spaces allowing also working (Di Marino & Lapintie, 2017; Koroma et al., 2014). This is again a working practice which is beneficial to the employer.

It seems, thus, that a theory of work that can deal with multi-locality needs to include in its analysis the new spatial arrangements of working that have emerged. It may be that failing to do so is related to the more general prioritizing of place against mobility, to the extent that 'workplace' is often used synonymously with 'employer' and 'job'. If we consider pre-industrial work, it also often needed synchronization and direct management: construction work had to be coordinated at the construction site, and music performances and rehearsals required the attendance of everyone at the same time. On the other hand, designers of the buildings did not need to present except in meetings and inspections, and composers could work at home. Both schedules and quality requirements were derived from the end products, not from presence or absence as such.

Thus, it seems that the reorganization of work more and more outside the assigned 'workplace' requires a new leadership and new kinds of work contracts in which the daily or weekly schedules give way to deadlines for the product to be finished or the service accomplished. Remuneration should also follow timely and high-quality deliverables, instead of mere presence at the workplace as much and with the results that are just above the minimum requirements set by the employer. If the employee is faster or more skilled, this could, thus, be rewarded with more leisure or higher salary. In this way, the new organization of work—instead of mimicking the office hours by keeping the employees alert—would return to product orientation. This could even potentially reduce the alienation that working-like-a-machine necessarily entails. This also means that the logic of presence and absence is historical. It takes time for the absence to disappear—to lose its connotations with laziness or non-commitment.

8   Heterotopia of the body

The dichotomies of urban/non-urban, permanent/temporary, and first/second home make it difficult to study and understand the meanings of the different places for people as part of their life-world. They will also easily lead us astray by forcing this subjective/objective reality into a conceptual framework that abstracts heavily from the actual experience. Consider, for instance, the practice of conflating second homes with tourism. The latter is based on a tacit assumption of one permanent address with an outside, a secondary or temporary environment. It is a sort of otherness that the permanent 'home' defines: we use our leisure time to get to know new places and cultures, sleeping in hotels, recreational vehicles, or tents, with the deliberate intention to leave them as soon as we have consumed the places. We go to see sights that are part of the commodification of places, we take selfies with these views as backgrounds: this is where I was, not where I am, not where I live. We buy souvenirs to remember (and 'prove') where we have been, but where we no longer are. As the name tells us, we are on a tour. Even if we would return to the same hotel or resort every year, temporariness is highlighted, although we are already moving in the grey zone between permanence and temporariness.

The reason for analysing second homes as a form of tourism is that they have originally been meant for vacation. But as we know, the dividing line between leisure and work has become blurred, and it has completely disappeared with the elderly who are retired and freed from geographical constraints. They may also go on a tour from their second home (where they spend most of their time), and it can hardly be understood as one of the destinations of their tour. The meaning is clearly different in terms of permanence, and, thus, including them in a homogeneous group of non-home destinations would be a case of violent abstraction.

Nevertheless, there is clearly some kind of otherness involved, both with respect to their relationship to 'first' homes and to their immediate environments. If the first home is in an urban environment, the second can in contrast be in a natural or rural environment. Or the other way round: a rural setting may be supplemented with an urban home near the services or workplaces. There are numerous ways that these contrasts or supplements

DOI: 10.4324/9781003124443-8

can structure themselves, and it is important to find conceptual frameworks that respect these differences. In this chapter, I shall attempt a reading of Foucault's concept of heterotopia to see whether it can give us a more nuanced way to analyse these differences between the various places and their environments. Heterotopia is a promising concept because it provides a possibility to address otherness as a 'worldly' feature, consistent with the corporeal philosophy developed in this book.

Nevertheless, heterotopia is also a contested concept. Foucault introduced it in a radio series and in a subsequent address to a group of architects and planners in 1967. He did not, however, elaborate it in his main corpus, and only just before his death he gave permission to publish the speech, called 'Des espaces autres' (Of other spaces) (Foucault, 1984). The text is far from unambiguous, and it has also been criticized for implying spatial totality and stasis. Arun Saldanha (2008) argues that the problem with the concept is that, at the time, Foucault had not yet distanced himself from the basic assumptions of structuralism. Thus, he could define heterotopia as sites 'in which the real sites, all the other real sites that can be found within the culture, are simultaneously represented, contested, and inverted'. This does indeed sound like a totality, and Saldanha is pessimistic about the possibilities to develop the concept into an analytical tool without such a commitment.

The incomplete form of Foucault's address gives perhaps too much liberty for interpretation, and it is sometimes difficult to see how the inferences from the text are made. For instance, Sacco et al. (2019) define heterotopia as 'the place where devices take shape: a portion of an autonomous, centripetal territory, separated from the rest of the world, a space that lives for itself and which is closed in itself', which is difficult to combine with Foucault's idea of representing, contesting and inverting other places. Otherness of a place, it seems, requires its outside, places from which it is different, and which determine its otherness. We may agree with Saldanha that these places do not need to be 'in relation with all the other sites' (Foucault, 1984, p. 3), or that this reflects a structuralist tendency. On the other hand, Foucault's characterization of them as places that are 'absolutely different from *all the sites that they reflect and speak about*' (ibid., p. 4, my italics) is less all-encompassing: heterotopia themselves mirror and represent *some* sites that are outside of them but determine their meaning. Heterotopia of deviation, for instance, can only be understood 'in relation to the required mean or norm' (ibid., p. 5).

I became interested in the potentiality of the concept through one of Foucault's several examples of heterotopia that he mentions, namely the Scandinavian sauna. According to Foucault, 'there are even heterotopias that are entirely consecrated to these activities of purification—purification that is partly religious and partly hygienic, such as the hammin of the Moslems, or else purification that appears to be purely hygienic, as in Scandinavian saunas' (Foucault, 1984, p. 7). The Scandinavian—or rather

Nordic—sauna is, however, much more complicated than this. Although historically it used to be the place for washing yourself in the countryside and also in working-class housing neighbourhoods in the cities (in public saunas of a neighbourhood), it lost its purely hygienic function a long time ago, as bathrooms became prevalent. Since saunas and the recreational homes connected to them apparently represent the largest form of residential multi-locality, it makes sense to consider whether a reformulated concept of heterotopia could shed light to this strangely resistant spatial phenomenon.

Foucault developed his concept from the concept of Utopia (actually the original radio series was on utopias), which is, as we know, a non-existent but good place at the same time. Being so, it suggests that reality as we know it is non-ideal, which also means that utopias need this mundane world as a platform from which they arise. As Foucault expresses it, 'they are sites that have a general relation of direct or inverted analogy with the real space of Society' (Foucault, 1986[1967]). Starting with Thomas More's *Utopia* from 1516 (More, 2003), utopias are often 'located' on an island that has clear borders inside of which the ideal rules of the society are maintained. In More's story the island was first connected to the mainland, but this connection had to be cut to guarantee the purity of its order. The existence of the Other, non-ideal world, however, is necessary. George Orwell placed his *Animal Farm* (1945) in a farm that was successfully defended against outside invasion from human farms.

As the fate of the revolutionary animals in Orwell's story demonstrated, there is only a small step from Utopia to Dystopia. This is because utopias don't include change or development, they are the end-point, the best possible world, and any change can only be a change for the worse. This means that the order has to maintained, if necessary, by force, and the revolution starts to eat its children. Yoko Ogawa's *The Memory Police* from 1994 is already a Dystopia from the start, and like More's it is located on an imaginary island where memory is step by step forbidden and destroyed, including the ferry that used to connect it to the mainland. Its message is important: without memory, the meanings of the forbidden and destroyed things are slowly fading away, until the people themselves fade away.

The historical utopias of urban planning carry with themselves these very same traits: they describe an intended end-state that does not include change or individual freedom to develop one's own interpretation of a good life. The industrialist and so-called Utopian socialist Robert Owen argued in 1813 of the necessity of developing a Utopian order in his book *Essays on the Formation of the Human Character*. Its aim was to remedy the condition of the characters of the workers, which were 'permitted to be very generally formed without proper guidance or direction, and, in many cases, under circumstances which directly impel them to a course of extreme vice and misery [...]' (Owen, 1813, p. 3). The tacit reference to the Platonic forms discussed earlier connects his work to the long history of totalitarian

Utopianism. Howard's Garden City and Social City are not so straightforward, but his town-country is still determining the physical structure and people's roles in its activities in detail. As Jane Jacobs ironically remarked, 'His aim was the creation of self-sufficient small towns, really very nice towns if you were docile and had no plans of your own and did not mind spending your life among others with no plans of their own. As in all utopias, the right to have plans of any significance belonged only to the planners in charge' (Jacobs, 1962, p. 17).

It is remarkable that even though utopias are in principle nowhere and the experiments to build them on earth have mainly been unsuccessful (even the Soviet Union from which the Animal Farm took its inspiration), they can still be seen behind many of the visions of urban planning. Consider, for instance, the neighbourhood by Kaitera described in Chapter 5, or the New Urbanist utopias around the world: they are not based on designing a process of urban development, or the degrees of freedom of individual citizens. It does not matter whether the models come from an imagined future or past, both forms of historicism describe an ideal end-state, and their failures result from real people not conforming (sic) to their norms and ideals.

How does Foucault's concept of heterotopia then relate to this Utopian tradition? The basic idea is that there are places with the similar characteristics as utopias, but which are still real places. They should, according to Foucault, represent a difference, an otherness (espaces autres): they should be 'counter-sites, a kind of effectively enacted utopia' in which other real sites are 'simultaneously represented, contested, and inverted'. This is far from clear, even if we forget that they should be related to 'all other sites'. In principle, we might consider that the planned and built utopias mentioned above (imagined ideal communities within a contained area like the one designed by Owen or Fourier or their contemporary followers) could represent 'enacted' utopias. They represent ideal end-states placed above a changing environment and acting people. Representation here must be indirect: the other place cannot exist without reference to this background, but since heterotopia are real, this inconsistency or juxtaposition must be part of its reality. The ideal, unchanging order of the utopia must constantly refer and justify itself in relation to its opposite, the chaos, the 'extreme vice and misery'. In this way, we might understand how heterotopia can 'contest and invert' the other real places.

Utopian plans and designs are, however, not examples that Foucault is using, and we may get carried away. Perhaps we should try to analyse his other examples in more detail before returning to the sauna and its context. His 'crisis heterotopias' are social spaces for individuals during an important period of change, danger or even vice: adolescents, menstruating women, pregnant women, the elderly, etc., are all very corporeal phases of human life with awakening sexuality, body fluids, and physical decay. These phases of highlighted corporeality could be closed from the rest of society which could then be closer to the ideal and unchanging order.

Foucault mentions the boarding school as one of the remnants of these crisis heterotopia: societies have difficulties in dealing with adolescents who are no longer children but not yet adults, and whose rising sexuality is seen as a potential vice. However, these heterotopias are disappearing, and their place is taken by 'heterotopias of deviation', where people deviating from the social norms are taken: rest homes, psychiatric hospitals, prisons, and—interestingly enough—retirement homes. The old age—again corporeal and constantly changing characteristic of human beings—can be seen on the borderline of deviation and crisis: compared to the healthy individuals, the elderly are all the time losing their physical and mental capacities but they also deviate from the industrial norm of work and leisure: unending leisure is idleness for the normal person. It is interesting that all these crisis- and deviant heterotopia are dealing with the body: the changing body, the bodily needs, the bodily fluids, the decaying body.

The second 'principal' that Foucault discusses is the change of the function of a specific heterotopia, and here he brings in the cemetery. Until the end of the eighteenth century, the cemetery was located in the middle of the town or village, beside the church, but when the belief in the immortal soul waned, the result was, paradoxically, a 'cult of the dead'. What he means by this is that, as we no longer believe in resurrection, the remains of the individual body become important; they are all that is left of us. On the other hand, this preoccupation with the body also made death an illness. The fear that the dead could infect the living made their existence in the middle of the town annoying, and the symbolic meaning of the cemetery changed dramatically. As a result, they started to be placed outside the city centres to suburbs, out of sight. There the individualized bodies can have their coffins or boxes of ashes. Curiously, we again end up with the body.

Foucault's third principle is that heterotopias are capable of juxtaposing several spaces that are in themselves incompatible. Natural examples are theatres and cinemas whose very function is to create illusions of spaces different from and far away from the rectangular room where they are shown. But a primordial example of such a heterotopia is the garden. A formal garden is a paradox in itself: it is made of natural elements that never cease to grow or wither and, thus, it needs constant maintenance by a gardener in order to preserve its charm. The abstract form and living nature are in a constant struggle: abstract rationality keeps the wild and untamed under its rule. But when this rule is weakened, nature always takes its course. Instead of this paradox, however, Foucault is more interested in the way the garden includes symbolically the whole world, and the carpet in its turn imitates the garden.

In the fourth principle, Foucault brings in time, 'heterochronies'. He uses the term 'slice of time', which seems to refer to the standard spatio-temporal understanding of time as a series of snapshots. This is one of the most controversial concepts in the text, criticized not only by Saldanha (2008) but many others, including myself, since it seems to entail both actualism and positivism. However, there might be an alternative reading (notwith-standing Foucault's less than precise expression). 'The heterotopia', he writes, 'begins to function at full capacity when men arrive at a sort of absolute break with their traditional time'. In addition to cemeteries, he mentions museums and libraries, 'constituting a place of all times that is itself outside of time and inaccessible to its ravages' (Foucault, 1986). This is indeed poorly expressed with time-slices as series of snapshots: as one enters and spends time (sic.) in these 'timeless' spaces, the time outside goes on, destroying and creating and, under capitalism, even melting all that is solid. The only change that is 'allowed' in museums and libraries is the constant accumulation of time, coexisting with other times. In 1967, when Foucault gave his speech, libraries were still physical spaces; the contem-porary libraries with their combination of physical and electronic books—or even only the latter—are different heterotopia, passing over the bodily experience of being in a timeless space. Even museums are nowadays pro-viding electronic access to their collections.

According to the fifth principle, the heterotopias presuppose a system of opening and closing, unlike public spaces. The entry may be compulsory, as in barracks or prisons, or voluntary but requiring rites and purification. To these types belong the Nordic saunas and—as I will argue—the second homes as a form of multi-locality. Before analysing them in detail, however, we can observe an interesting thing which is not always noticed in the liter-ature on heterotopia. Even though Foucault uses the term 'counter-site', the examples that he uses are by no means deviant (only places *for* the deviant), challenging or revolutionary: boarding schools, psychiatric hospitals, pris-ons, retirement homes, gardens, libraries, museums, Moslems' hammins, and Nordic saunas are all established and 'accepted' social spaces with established practices and rites connected to them (who and how to enter, how to dress, how to behave, what to do, how to leave, etc.). Even the brothel that he mentions can be seen as a place of 'tamed' sexuality. Thus, they are not counter-sites to the established social order, rather they are part of it. Their functions can change over time, as the cemeteries losing their central position in the urban structure, but not as a result of any coun-ter movement. In the literature on heterotopias, this concept of counter-site has, however, been given a very different meaning.

According to Edwards and Bulkeley (2017), for instance, heterotopias are 'spaces defined by their otherness to the society in which they are located [...] real spaces which challenge modes of thinking, which embody in them-selves the changes required to reorder society'. They 'also contain the inten-tion to enact transformation towards a better future'. According to Ntounis and Kanellopoulou (2017), 'heterotopias represent spatial otherness, inject a touch of alterity into the sameness of everyday life, and disrupt our perception of normality within a given culture and the environment that surrounds an area'. The authors give rather different examples of hetero-topia than those of Foucault: squats, brothels, rave parties and cannabis festivals. This is how they characterize 'jurisdictional heterotopias', which can, on the other hand, be normalized, as in their cases of Christiania and Metelkova. Kevin Hetherington has also interpreted the heterotopia as an alternative ordering of society: 'Heterotopias are spaces in which an alternative social ordering is performed. These are spaces in which a new way of ordering emerges that stands in contrast to the taken-for-granted mundane idea of social order that exists within society' (Hetherington, 1997, p. 40).

These interpretations seem to me, if not the exact opposite of what Foucault was trying to say, at least far from it. Considering that Foucault was a philosopher of power rather than freedom or emancipation, and that neither Utopias nor heterotopias are devoid of power, it is difficult to find justification for the 'revolutionary' interpretation of an alternative social order or ordering from the text itself. If 'there is probably not a single culture in the world that fails to constitute heterotopias', they seem to be necessary parts of the social order, not its opposites. This is of course a challenging theoretical idea: what does it mean to represent otherness within the social order of the culture and still be part of it? On the other hand, production of Otherness has always been an essential part of human cultures. In the other text on heterotopias, the preface to *The Order of Things*, heterotopias are admittedly different, characterized as disturbing, undermining language, and destroying syntax (Foucault, 1985a, p. xviii).

Foucault's reflections can, thus, give inspiration for very different interpretations. Leaving aside what Foucault 'really' meant, or whether that is a relevant question, I would like to continue my contrasting analysis of heterotopia as 'established otherness'. This will make it possible to use it for understanding strong cultural spaces and practices, such as saunas and second homes. It is also interesting that Foucault's heterotopias seem to have a strong connection to the human body, to its carnal existence. The deviant people are closed from 'normal' space as bodies, the heterotopia of crisis refers to temporary stages of the body or its final decay.

This bodily dimension is also relevant in the experience of the Nordic sauna. Undressing is the entrance rite to this quasi-sacred space, making one exposed to the elements on nature: hot air and steam, cool air and cold water—for the bravest even snow and ice. Being naked also means being exposed to other people, but in a de-sexualized space. 'Being naked' is often symbolically connected with honesty, openness and unpretentiousness, but in the sauna this connection is physical. When you are unable to build your image with clothes, make-up, jewellery, wrist-watch, or other devices, your ordinary identity is temporarily put on hold and simplified. This is probably why it is easier to 'open your soul' while bathing.

The sauna as a particular space (with an internal structure of benches, water and oven) and a particular social practice (warming the space, undressing yourself, throwing water on the oven to produce steam, taking a steam bath, cooling, perhaps swimming, and doing it all over again) has stayed alive through urbanization, modernization, and individualization.

There are small saunas connected to bathrooms in urban apartments but also larger saunas for social gatherings. The public saunas that almost disappeared have also experienced a renaissance with modernistic buildings covering a medieval social practice. They are still connected with bathing, but the hygienic function has become secondary. What is remarkable in saunas is that the they pierce social strata, from working class families and sports teams to business leaders and politicians. Earlier, when there were few women in high positions, even political and business negotiations could take place in a sauna.

The sauna is also an elemental part of the recreational homes that started with small and simple summer cottages, affordable to the middle and even working-class families. At the same time when urban housing was upscaled in the cities in the wake of the welfare-state, the first post-war summer cottages were very modest: without running water or sewage, without electricity, with very small spaces to sleep in—but always with a sauna. Thus, the summer cottage represented an 'other space' where urbanized families voluntarily retreated to lead a simple life close to nature.

Another interesting feature of the summer cottage and its descendants is its curious relationship with time. One might think that they are temporary places only visited during summer vacations or weekends, compared to the 'permanent' home in the city. However, their repeated use and geographical location can also represent stability compared to the changing places of urban living. Since you don't need to commute daily from the cottage to your workplace, it is more independent of distances and, therefore, a potential place for telecommuting. Staying in the cottage is, in a way, timeless time, with a recurring rhythm of enjoyment that does not lead anywhere. But this enjoyment can only be understood as juxtaposed to the world outside with its expectations, obligations and devouring time.

With this interpretation, we may avoid the problems related to the 'slices of time'. Instead of considering them in the positivist sense as constellations of physical things ('space') following each other in time, we may indeed see that 'heterotopia begins to function at full capacity when men arrive at a sort of absolute break with their traditional time'. These may be the 'enacted utopia' that multi-local people are building for themselves, an absolute break with their rational but ravaging daily existence.

9   The city of cyborgs

Reference to human characteristics and needs is evidently the most widely used argument for planning and policy proposals—and also critique of them. For many, it seems almost a self-evident argument, since its opposite, designing, and planning *in*human environments is unthinkable, at least as an objective. The concepts 'human', 'humane', and 'humanism' have positive connotations even if they would remain undefined. We should plan cities 'for people', 'for the human being', we are told. The man is the measure of good cities.

The problem with this humanistic declaration is that 'the human being' does not exist—at least not as a material being. It exists only as a construction, as an artefact. This construction, however, can only be done through abstraction, a politico-historical process whereby certain elements are deemed to be essential to human beings and, thus, worthy of our attention and safeguarding. The other characteristics, those that are judged contingent or special are considered inferior to the generalized human being. Thus, the actual, corporeal human beings are stripped of major part of their characteristics—stripped naked, literally. However, the result of this process is not general but special, such as the famous *uomo universalis* by Leonardo: white, male, young, fit. It is an easy target for posthuman critique: feminist, post-colonial, or queer arguments can justly claim that this kind of construction is simply the result of dominant ideologies and taken-for-granted normalization (e.g. Braidotti, 2013).

Mark Johnson takes us a step further by quoting a poem by Billy Collins: 'Then I remove my flesh and hang it over a chair/I slide it off my bones like a silken garment/I do this so that what I write will be pure'. (Johnson, 2007, p. 2). Indeed, why stop at the naked body? On the other hand, stripping particular human beings of some of their special characteristics does not make them representatives of other special characteristics: black do not become white, homosexual straight, or women men, even if 'man' also refers to this abstracted, generalized human being. Rejecting every feature that is contingent in a human being will simply end up losing the whole thing. In this sense, the human being really does not exist.

How could it, then, be the most important source of legitimacy in planning and urban policies? It would be too easy to conclude that we are *actually*

DOI: 10.4324/9781003124443-9

planning our cities for white, male, young, and healthy human beings, and only *pretend* that we are planning them for the generalized human being (which does not exist, but nobody notices). We do take into account many special and contingent features by taking care of, for instance, the safety of children and women, the accessibility of the disabled and elderly persons, or the health effects of air-borne particles to people with cardiovascular disease. We also try to avoid socio-economic and racial segregation. Some special features are, evidently, more special than others, even if they represent Otherness. Paradoxically, humanism seems to require exactly that.

In addition to these problems related to human diversity, it is also difficult to include technology in humanistic essentialism. The technologies that humans have taken to use have varied throughout history, and they have had tremendous impacts on human activities, social relations, forms of production, consumption, and mobility. However, technology is naturally contingent, and it would be difficult to justify any one type of technology to be necessarily included in our conception of humanity. On the other hand, it would be difficult to argue that some specific amount of technology that we use would make us non-human.

It is important not to confuse this conceptual problem with the question on the posthuman and transhuman condition. For instance, Søren Holm states that 'The term posthuman strictly speaking only connotes individuals that are in some way descendants from humans, but are no longer human, whereas transhuman connotes individuals who possess abilities that are beyond human abilities', such as life expectancy of more than 500 years, twice the cognitive capacities of humans, or near-complete control over the sensory input (Holm, 2017, referring to Nick Bostrom). This kind of bio-technological improvement naturally opens the question of when these beings are 'no longer human', but in order to think about it, one first needs a definition of 'human'. Multi-local people using information and communication technology as part of their daily life do not have such powers, but their humanity still lacks an essentialist definition. In history, many groups of people that we now keep human have lacked this property, according to the ruling classes. Thus, the definition seems to be political rather than logical, and the same is undeniably true of the mainly biological features that are supposed to bring legitimacy to our planning solutions.

Traditional language used in planning and politics may be misleading in this respect, since we may speak of designing cities for 'pedestrians' instead of 'cars'—as if they would not be simply human beings using different technologies. Even pedestrians are usually not naked but use clothes, shoes, and umbrellas, while people using cars use coachwork, tyres, and windshields for the same purposes. Neither technology is human as such, but they are used by human beings, who do not thereby lose their humanity. The same is obviously true of people using mobile phones, laptops, and wi-fi networks. Prioritizing one technology over another has to be given another justification. Finding such justification to promote pedestrian-friendly cities, for instance, is certainly possible. Unequal use of space, inefficient investment in infrastructure, difficulties in providing services, or health effects can be used as such arguments, but they are also political, not logical arguments. The problem with humanistic justification is exactly that it hides the political nature of urbanism.

We could perhaps try to study the hidden premises of humanistic urban planning by analysing more in detail how these arguments are developed. One of the most well-known ideologists of humanistic planning, or 'planning for people', is Jan Gehl, who has tried to infer planning principles from our knowledge of the psychology and biology of human beings. According to him, the modernistic urban planners failed because they knew 'virtually nothing' of the human being. But what kind of knowledge could it be, considering the difficulties in trying to define humanity? Gehl is not attempting to develop his ideas theoretically, his intention has rather been to give guidelines to planners and politicians who want to create pedestrian-friendly cities—or actually, pedestrian-friendly city centres, since the problems of city regions are not discussed by him. However, Gehl has been very influential and, thus, deserves to be discussed—particularly as he attempts to base his doctrines on science.

In his most influential book *Cities for People* (2010), and the consultancy behind it, Gehl takes the human being to be the 'customer' of urban planners and designers. This customer is 'a linear, frontal, horizontal, maximum 5 km/h – 3 mph human being' (p. 32). Interestingly, in the book he uses a photograph of 'Laura, aged 1', with only diapers on and shoes in her hands. This is pretty close to the 'naked' human being discussed earlier, but technology is already creeping like a snake to the paradise. The point in this definition is obvious: if we can pick the characteristics of human beings to make them *the* human being, we can justify our planning solutions—and criticize planning failures—based on these features. The argument is that the evolution that has created *homo sapiens* from the previous extinct hominoids has been very slow, compared to the cultural and technological evolution of humankind: 'Twenty-first century urban pedestrians are the result of an evolution over millions of years. Man has evolved to move slowly and on foot, and the human body is linear in orientation [...] In short, Homo sapiens is a linear, frontal, horizontally oriented upright mammal. Paths, streets and boulevards are all spaces for linear movement designed on the basis of the human locomotor system' (ibid., p. 33).

The problem with the argument is, however, that this creature of the slow evolution is also able to use the technology available, with exactly the same perceptual and locomotive apparatus that she is using while walking. We can use cars (120 km/h), airplanes (800 km/h), and even rockets (28 000 km/h), if only we find or create spaces for them. Pedestrian paths and streets are indeed created for the slow pace of walking, but evolution itself does not prevent us from moving faster. This also means that juxtaposing 'pedestrians' against 'cars' is not very informative, since the latter gives access to a dramatically larger region that the former. It is possible—and often advisable—to 'get rid of cars' in the city centres, but there is no turning back from the increasing accessibility created by modern technology.

Global access to information 'wherever you are' is, however, different from the physical accessibility provided by machines moving ever faster. Paradoxically, this new accessibility can even support the urban renewal that Gehl and his followers are promoting—but for different reasons. Gehl's idea is that, as social animals, human beings need to be able to perceive one another's moods and activities in order to form social relationships, something which they long for. This requires not only the slow movement by walking but also incentives to stop and socialize. He famously divided human activities to necessary (e.g. going to work or school), optional (walking slowly down the promenade, stopping to watch the scenery, etc.), and social (including all kinds of contact between people in city space). Theoretically this does not hold water, of course, since there are hardly any necessary human activities 'with no choice' (ibid., p. 18): you can be out of school, telecommute or choose a different route. On the other hand, the Simmelian blasé attitude towards other people on the street is also a social activity, safeguarding one's mental capacity to concentrate on meaningful social relationships. This does not require stopping, rather to the contrary. After the mobile phones became widely used equipment of everyday life, the use of public spaces has changed dramatically. Instead of talking to each other (which one would expect if 'man is man's greatest joy'), people are mostly staring at their smartphones, creating a bubble of non-contact around themselves—at the same time as they are connected to their friends wherever they are. Technology changes the way that people—as human beings—form their social relationships. Even without transhuman abilities, we are already 'cyborgs', essentially technology-animals.

10 Conclusion

From places to lifescapes

This book has been an exploration through a wide terrain of scholarship and practice. Its intention has not been to give an overview of anything, flying over a large territory in order to describe its features, mapping them for a more efficient locating of human bodies and their movements. From high above, we may see people—to quote Borges and his 'Chinese encyclopedia' discussed by Foucault (1985a)—as animals that 'from a long way off look like flies'. The mind can distance itself from its object, stripping it from the multitude of its characteristics, abstracting it as an object of knowledge and power. The flies keep moving and changing their place, too fast for the scholarly eye to follow. If they cannot be trapped or killed—which is of course an option adopted by totalitarian governments as well as biologists—a new creature has to be constructed, one that stays put in its place, knows its place and allows its place to be known. It is registered in a permanent or temporary address, and it moves slowly, 'urbanizing' or 'ruralizing' itself. It does not oppose the pigeon-holing of the researcher: it is a man, a woman or other, homeless, middle-class, aged, married or unhappy. At the same time, people of flesh and blood are developing their own epistemologies of escape. They are hunted by predators interested in their money or their political opinions, but there is always more than meets the eye.

One of the problems of research on multi-locality is that it is sliced into smaller pieces, ending up marginalising the phenomenon or positioning it inside a chosen field of research. One may be interested in summer cottages as a form of tourism, disregarding that they are more stable and used also for other purposes. One may be interested in those who rent an apartment near their workplace while their family stays behind, disregarding them if it appears that there are not so many of them. Or one may be interested in those who telecommute from home, disregarding the many other places that can be used. Or even if one studies residential multi-locality, work, and other purposes in life are kept outside.

Considering multi-locality as a wider phenomenon—to the extent that we are all more or less multi-local—is of course risky, since the concept may start losing its sharpness. Nevertheless, I think that this risk needs to be taken, instead of excluding possible types of multi-locality at the

DOI: 10.4324/9781003124443-10

outset. In this book, I have considered several such types, many of which are not usually regarded as multi-locality, such as homeless or commuters. The main criterion that I have used is that multi-local people use several places and movement between them—including possible movement—as an important part of their life. The rhythm of this movement can be daily, weekly, monthly or even less (such as those who have a permanent residence in one country and a second home in another). This opens several theoretical and methodological challenges.

The primary example of such challenge is the fact that statistics—as the state or Royal science *par excellence*—is not able to follow the corporeal human beings and, thus, fails to know their location and actual movements. Not knowing is not a problem as such, since our knowledge is always limited and fallible. The problem only arises if we tacitly assume that a corporeal human being, her location and movement, *can* be known with statistics, so that the mind-body would coincide with the statistical unit, being ontologically the same. However, the mind-body moves freely within the neighbourhood where it is registered, within the municipality, across municipal borders, in several urban regions, and even in several countries. The case of the couple moving in a triangle according to seasons in three countries shows how artificial the assumption of one place of residence is.

Interestingly, this problem is usually not even discussed in research using statistical data as its main source. It seems that this information is reified, as if there would be a man respecting the statistical information. In a sense, there is a dual ontology of the corporeal mind-body and the statistical state-man who are essentially different, even belonging to different ontological classes (material things versus mental constructions). When the corporeal mind-body goes to work, the state-man stays behind at home. This is serious, since the imaginary collection of state-men allows planners and policy-makers to imagine a container where these artificial state-men are located, and where they need to be provided with services, such as schools, health care, parks, or shops. The most recent imaginary planning idea is the 'fifteen minutes city', where all daily needs should be reached by 'sustainable modes of transport', walking, cycling or public transport. But what is the centre of this fifteen minutes region for the citizen? Obviously, the place where the state-man 'lives'. The absurdity of this concept is revealed only by considering a (corporeal) man who works in the city but cannot afford to buy an apartment there, and he needs to travel for forty-five minutes from a suburb. Should he quit his job to remain inside the 15 minutes radius?

This dual ontology is also problematic because it tacitly entails a normative stance, according to which staying is morally superior to moving. This long-standing ideology against vagabondage has been built with movies, books, and policies. We should become 'rooted' in one place and community, participate in the development of our neighbourhood, have close relationships with our neighbours, etc. Forcing or persuading to stay is, however, an essential form of modern power. As sociologist Timo Kalanti writes, referring to Foucault: 'Restrictions are targeted at places, and governance is realized by forcing to stay put. That is why being on the move is being beyond reach, between places, nowhere. The movement has to be stopped, if the mover is aimed to be a subject of discipline. Paraphrasing Michel Foucault, stopping is not only the condition of controlling power, it is precisely the form through which disciplinary power is realized' (Kalanti, 2009, my translation).

Failing to see this dual ontology and its implications may result in excluding the spatiality that does not correspond to the norm of one home, one (nuclear) family and standard rhythm of life. If one uses, for instance, official statistics of the primary residence and tries to find other places of everyday or weekly activity, one ends up adopting the traditional conceptions of family, place of residence and 'other' places (Hasanzadeh et al., 2021). However, one may ask whether these concepts of 'places individuals visit during a typical week' make much sense in the context of multi-locality. What is a typical week? How many times in a week do you have to visit a place to call it 'everyday'? Every day, several times in a week, once in a week? What about the places one visits seldom, like the opera? What about the weekends? As we remember, some people may spend most of their weekends and their holidays in their second homes. Some people—for instance those who are already retired—may spend most of their days and nights in the second homes, even though it is not their formal address. These differences are perhaps not problematic if we study the population, not people, and statistics as the state-science is dedicated to the study of population. On the other hand, population is the primary object of biopolitics interested in the health and productivity of groups of people.

It seems that, in addition to the corporeal person, we need to make other extensions to our ontology. Even if we could follow the movement of people between different places and the time and rhythm of using them (e.g. with mobile phone data or surveys asking them where they have been and why), we would still reach only a fragment of the multi-local urban experience. The city is not something that merely happens, or flows. We don't only follow the route of a bus, we may *take* it to reach our destination—or we may *not* take it and walk or take a taxi instead. We may go to the movies, but we can also choose not to and stay at home. The city, the urban space, is full of such opportunities that we may call potentialities, that is, possibilities that are within our reach (financially, physically, socially, culturally). We only pick some of them, but the others don't disappear just because we don't use the opportunity. The city and our life in it don't only consist of actualities that can be observed and measured, but also potentialities that we can know and experience. Unlike the state-men, these potentialities are not imaginary. It is part of the bus and myself as material things, as well as the rules and routes of public transport, that the bus can be taken or not taken. The potential places near and far are the landscape that we have around us, not only the routine mobility between certain places that we perhaps have. Failing to see and appreciate these potentialities in research is what could be called *actualism*.

Philosophers have been busy in studying the logic of these possibilities and the related concepts, so-called *modal* concepts. Since we don't know everything in the city (what we can do or what can happen), our knowledge is restricted and fallible (we may mistakenly believe that something can happen). Our knowledge gives us only a small subset of urban space, as the space of possibilities—but even this subset is much larger than what we actually do or what can happen. Hintikka has called them *alternatives*. The things we know, what we can do or what can happen are our *epistemic alternatives*. If we add to this our beliefs (including the mistaken ones), we can call this larger subset *doxastic alternatives*. Similarly, our limited capacities to perceive, remember people and places give as the corresponding set of alternatives (*perceptual* and *mnemonic* alternatives). Since the city is also a normative space, there are a lot of alternatives that are allowed and also those that are prohibited: *deontic* alternatives.

We shall not discuss modal logic or possible worlds semantics any further, but the main thing to be taken from it is that our urban experience (which necessarily includes knowledge, beliefs, perceptions, memories, and ideas of what we should do or shouldn't do) is not closed to the actual deeds and events. Consequently, the places where we don't go are still there, as potential places where we *could* go. We don't just follow our own movement between places, or that of others, but we navigate among these several alternatives. Thus, studying, for instance, daily or weekly mobility between two places of residence does not give us the whole picture, far from it.

The third extension that we need to make in our ontology is to add the dimension of negativity or absence to the positivity or presence. This is relevant to multi-locality, since—as already Hägerstrand argued—we cannot be physically present in two places, and in order to be present in one place, we need to be absent in others. Being absent—negativity—is, however, not the same as being present in another place. Absence is an existing fact, something that other people can observe, and to which they can develop an attitude. It may be condemnation, wonder, worry, or relief. This is particularly relevant when we are considering multi-locality of work. Traditionally, even information-intensive work has required presence at a certain place at certain times—the fact that inspired Hägerstrand to develop his famous 'prism'. Controlling presence has been the major part of management of work in the workplace, and actually the term 'workplace' reveals the presupposition that working is happening at a certain place. This presence has been essentially connected with time, determining usually the compensation for the work of the employee.

All this changed dramatically when virtual presence became possible. Actually, the traditionally demanded presence at the workplace, controlled visually, could have been questioned even earlier, if the management and leadership of employers had adopted control mechanisms based on results. Forced by the sudden outbreak of the pandemic, employers had no excuses left, and teleworking had to be allowed if only the task allowed it. In principle this did not mean a dramatic change in working practices: meetings were replaced by teleconferences, and tasks that did not require interaction were accomplished as before. Time wasted for travelling diminished but, unfortunately, also informal encounters between co-workers.

Spatially, on the other hand, the change has been more dramatic. The two places, home and workplace, have lost their previous taken-for-granted positions as the starting points and destinations of everyday life: going to work, returning back home. The absence from home when at work used to be total, and doing too much overtime could even risk losing one's marriage. In hybrid work, in contrast, home can become an office, and office more a meeting place. Presence and absence get mixed: it may be necessary to divide the home into more or less intimate parts, resembling the traditional combined workshops and living spaces of craftsmen and small entrepreneurs or professionals. Telework is a form of distributed work: large organizations, 'factories' of office work, are spatially distributed to hundreds of spaces not controlled by the corporations.

Upon reflection, it is beginning to look like the starting point of our examination—a person moving from one place to another for working or living—is too simple and restrictive. If people don't simply move but have a whole variety of different potential places to choose from, with different meanings connected to them *and* the fact that all these alternatives are there, perhaps we need a more suitable concept. Brigitte Jordan used the term 'lifescape' to refer to the blurring boundaries between work ('workscape') and other activities in life, as well as between physical and virtual (Jordan, 2009). In her autobiographical analysis (Jordan, 2008), she also described how working and living intermingle in her two home/workplaces in Springhill (California) and Besos del Viento (Costa Rica). Although there have been several 'scapes' in literature—paraphrasing the more common landscape and townscape—this concept may prove to be more fruitful that simply the multi-locality that we have been working with so far. If we consider landscape, for instance, it is clearly not a collection of places and movements between them. There are, of course, places from which we look at the scenery, the vistas, and there is a long tradition of landscape painting. Real landscapes, however, are something that we move within, as bodies, and this experience is modal: the landscape opens before us, giving us possibilities to move and also experience our mortality and change.

However, the blurring boundaries is not necessarily the best way to characterize lifescapes as they are emerging in the contemporary societies. It is true that traditional work within the factory-offices was based on boundaries, as both workplace and worktime determined the authority of the employer. But what was outside these spaces and times? And what is inside and outside now? The problem is that in order to have blurring boundaries, you need to have boundaries, and you need to be able to determine the topological space that is 'far enough' from these blurring boundaries to be something and not the other. Life, for one, has only two boundaries, birth and death, and they are not blurred. Inside the space of life, there is work and other activities, there is leisure, there is travelling, and more. What happens when work is distributed? Life has always been distributed, work-life has been life as well, even if it has been spatially and temporarily contained. If being inside the employee's premises—being present—is not the definition of work anymore, this also means that the life outside the workplace and worktime is no longer sovereign space of the employer, in spite of the more developed control of presence. In fact, there have always been borderline spaces between home and the workplace, namely travelling to and from work. This non-free free time has become more and more important, as growing cities and mega-regions have forced employees to travel long distances to reach their workplace, or alternatively rent a work apartment in the city.

These space-times are the ones that seem to be evaporating, as work is divorced from place—albeit only for those whose tasks are not space- or place-bound. But we should not hasten to say that this means emancipation. Although contiguity has lost its dominance, synchrony perhaps has not. Thousands of former office workers have experienced continuous series of teleconferences, where their virtual presence is required. Those who can concentrate on doing their work uncontrolled, whenever and wherever they want, still seem to be a small elite of experts. Thus, we cannot avoid analysing the power relationships of this new spatial configuration—at worst it can mean that work colonizes the lifeworld of employees.

It seems, thus, that a theoretical understanding of multi-locality cannot be satisfied with a set of places visited more or less often, and the psychological and social meanings attached to them. The landscape ahead of our subjects, as corporeal mind-bodies, has to include the alternatives that they can imagine, know and prepare for. Changing places and being on the move—and also having the ability to do so—is not simply a rational or forced process, but a heavily cultural and political one, in which the mind-bodies encounter local norms and values, and in which their absence from other places—real negativity—also has impacts on their social identity. Developing a theory from this perspective—including my own accomplishment—is still fragmentary, necessarily wandering in an uncharted territory, manned by separate established disciplines. The research on the challenges that the concept of multi-locality—and the more extensive concept of lifescape—presents us is not only critical towards existing theories and empirical results, but it also needs to gather the elements that are useful for such an integrated approach.

References

Allen, T.D. & Goldern, T.D. & Shockley, K.M. (2015). How Effective Is Telecommuting? Assessing the Status of Our Scientific Findings. *Psychological Science in the Public Interest*, Vol. 16(2), 40–68.

Anderson, B. (2006). *Imagined Communities. Reflections on the Origin and Spread of Nationalism*. London and New York: Verso.

Austin, J.L. (1962). *How to Do Things with Words: The William James Lectures Delivered at Harvard University in 1955*. Edited by J.O. Urmson and Marina Sbisà. Oxford: Clarendon Press.

Bhaskar, R. (1993). *Dialectic. The Pulse of Freedom*. London and New York: Verso.

Birch, E.L. & Wachter, S.M. (2011). *Global Urbanization*. Philadelphia, PA: University of Pennsylvania Press.

Braidotti, R. (2013). *The Posthuman*. Cambridge and Malden: Polity Press.

Brenner, N. (2018). Debating Planetary Urbanization: For an Engaged Pluralism. *Environment and Planning D: Society and Space*, Vol. 36(3), 570–590.

Castells, M. (1977). *The Urban Question. A Marxist Approach*. Translated by Alan Sheridan. London: Edward Arnold.

Castells, M. (2000). *The Rise of the Network Society*, 2nd Edition. Malden, Oxford and Carlton: Blackwell Publishing.

Chemero, A. & Turvey, M.T. (2007). Complexity, Hypersets, and the Ecological Perspective on Perception-Action. *Biological Theory*, Vol. 2(1), 23–36.

Davoudi, S. & Brooks, E. (2020). City-Regional Imaginaries and Politics of Rescaling. *Regional Studies*, Vol. 55(1), 52–62.

Delcore, H.D. (2018). The Lifescapes of Public University Students: Extending Work Practice to Macro and Micro Levels. *Human Organization*, Vol. 77(1), 1–9.

Deleuze, G. & Quattari, F. (2019). *A Thousand Plateaus*. London and New York: Bloomsbury Academic.

Di Marino, M. & Lapintie, K. (2015). Libraries as Transitory Work-Spaces and Spatial Incubators. *Library and Information Science Research*, Vol. 37, 118–129.

Di Marino, M. & Lapintie, K. (2017). Emerging Workplaces in Post-Functionalist Cities. *Journal of Urban Technology*, DOI: 10.1080/10630732.2017.1297520.

Di Marino, M. & Lilius, J. & Lapintie, K. (2018). New Forms of Multi-Local Working: Identifying Multi-Locality in Planning as Well as Public and Private organizations' Strategies in the Helsinki Region. *European Planning Studies*, Vol. 26(10), 2015–2035.

Dionne, G. & Dostie, B. (2007). New Evidence on the Determinants of Absenteeism Using Linked Employer-Employee Data. *Industrial and Labor Relations Review*, Vol. 61(1), 108–120.

Edwards, G.A. & Bulkeley, H. (2017). Heterotopia and the Urban Politics of Climate Change Experimentation. *Environment and Planning D: Society and Space*, Vol. 36(2), 350–369.

Elliott, J.R. & Clements, M.T. (2014). Urbanization and Carbon Emissions: A Nationwide Study of Local Counterveiling Effects in the United States. *Social Science Quarterly*, Vol. 95(3), 795–816.

Engels, F. (2005). *The Condition of the Working Class in England*. Salt Lake City, UT: Project Gutenberg. https://www.gutenberg.org/ebooks/17306.

Faludi, A. (2013). Territorial Cohesion, Territorialism, Territoriality, and Soft Planning: A Critical Review. *Environment and Planning A*, Vol. 45(6), 1302–1317.

Faludi, A. (2018). *The Poverty of Territorialism: A Neo-Medieval View of Europe and European Planning*. Cheltenham: Edward Elgar Publishing.

Foucault, M. (1985a). *The Order of Things. An Archaeology of the Human Sciences*. London: Tavistock.

Foucault, M. (1985b). *The Archaeology of Knowledge*. London: Tavistock.

Foucault, M. (1986[1967]). Of Other Spaces. *Diacritics*, Vol. 16(1), pp. 22–27. Translated by Jay Miskowiec from "Des Espaces Autres", March 1967.

Foucault, M. (1997). *Ethics. Subjectivity and Truth*. Edited By Paul Rabinow, New York, NY: The New York Press.

Foucault, M. (2004). *"The Society must Be Defended". Lectures at the Collège de France, 1975–76*. Translated by David Macey. London: Penguin Books.

Galileo. (1623). Il Saggiatore. *Opere*, Vol. VI, p. 232.

Gajendran, R.S. & Harrison, D. (2007). The Good, the Bad, and the Unknown about Telecommuting: Meta-Analysis of Psychological Mediators and Individual Consequences. *Journal of Applied Psychology*, Vol. 92(6), 1524–1540.

Gehl, J. (2010). *Cities for People*. Washington, Covelo and London: Island Press.

Gibson, J. (1986). *The Ecological Approach to Visual Perception*. Mahwah, NJ: Lawrence Erlbaum Associates, Inc. (Original work published 1979.)

Glaeser, E. (2011). *Triumph of the City. How Our Greatest Invention Makes Us Richer, Smarter, Greener, Healthier, and Happier*. New York, NY: Penguin Books.

Gogol, N. (2004). Dead Souls. New York, NY: Penguin Books

Habermas, J. (1981). *Knowledge and Human Interests*. 2nd Edition. London: Heinemann.

Haggett, P. (1979). *Geography. A Modern Synthesis*. New York, NY: Harper & Row.

Harvey, D. (2004, 29 May). Space as a Key Word. Paper for Marx and Philosophy Conference. Institute of Education, London. http://frontdeskapparatus.com/files/harvey2004.pdf

Harvey, D. (2009). *Social Justice and the City*. Athens: University of Georgia Press

Hasanzadeh, K. & Kyttä, M. & Lilius, J. & Ramezani, S. & Rinne, T. (2021). Centricity and Multi-Locality of Activity Spaces: The Varying Ways Young and Old Adults Use Neighbourhoods and Extra-Neighbourhood Spaces in Helsinki Metropolitan Area. *Cities*, Vol. 110.

Helsinki City Plan. (2013). *Vision 2050. Urban plan: The New Helsinki City Plan*. Helsinki: Reports by the Helsinki City Planning Department general planning unit 2013:23

Hetherington, K. (1997). *The Badlands of Modernity. Heterotopia and Social Ordering.* London: Routledge.

Hintikka, J. (1969). Models for Modalities. Selected Essays. *Synthese Library*, Vol. 23. Netherlands: Springer.

Holliday, I. (2002). Is the British State Hollowing Out? *The Political Quarterly*, Vol. 71(2), 162–176.

Holm, S. (2017). Evaluating the Posthuman Future – Some Philosophical Problems. *European Review*, Vol. 25(1), 131–139.

Huffman, T.T. & Leiuer, C. & Generous, M.A. & Hinrichs, M.M. & Brenneman, L. (2021). Climbing the 'Scaffolded City': Tactics Used by Homeless Young Adults to Navigate Employment Barriers. *Journal of Applied Communication Research*, Vol. 49(2), 148–167.

Hutchison, R. (2010). Urbanization. Edited By Hutchinson, R., *Encyclopedia of Urban Studies*. Thousand Oakes, CA: Sage.

Hägerstrand, T. (1970). What about People in Regional Science? *Papers of the Regional Science Association*, Vol. 24, 7–21.

Hägerstrand, T. (1977). The Impact of Social Organization and Environment upon the Time-Use of Individuals and Households. *Social Issues in Regional Policy and Planning*, Vol. 27, 59–68.

ILO. (2021). *Teleworking arrangements during the COVID-19 crisis and beyond.* Paper prepared for the 2nd Employment Working Group Meeting under the 2021 Italian Presidency of the G20.

Iwata, S. & Karato, K. (2011). Homeless Networks and Geographic Concentration: Evidence from Osaka City. *Papers in Regional Science*, Vol. 90(1), 27–46.

Jacobs, J. (1962). *The Death and Life of Great American Cities.* London: Jonathan Cape.

Jacobs, J.E. (2010). A Powers Theory of Modality: Or, How I Learned to Stop Worrying and Reject Possible Worlds. *Philosophical Studies*, Vol. 151, 227–248.

Jedwah, R. & Christiaensen, L. & Gindelsky, M. (2017). Demography, Urbanization and Development: Rural Push, Urban Pull and … Urban Push. *Journal of Urban Economics*, Vol. 98, 6–16.

Johnson, M. (2007). *The Meaning of the Body. Aesthetics of Human Understanding.* Chicago & London: The University of Chicago Press.

Jordan, B. (2008). Living a Distributed Life: Multilocality and Working at a Distance. *NAPA Bulletin*, Vol. 30(1), 28–55.

Jordan, B. (2009). Blurring Boundaries: The "Real" and the "Virtual" in Hybrid Spaces. *Human Organization*, Vol. 68(2), 181–193.

Kaitera, H. (1982). *Työpaikat ja asuinympäristö.* Espoo: Otakustantamo.

Kalanti, T. (2009). *Ruumis ja rauta. Esseitä esineiden sosiaalisuudesta (The body anf the iron. Essays on the sociality of things).* Helsinki: Helsingin yliopiston sosiologian laitoksen tutkimuksia, n:o 259.

Koroma, J. & Hyrkkänen, U. & Vartiainen, M. (2014). Looking for People, Places and Connections: Hindrances When Working in Multiple Locations: A Review. *New Technology, Work & Employment*, Vol. 29(2), 139–159.

Kramer, C. (2012). 'Alles hat Seine Zeit' – die 'Time Geography' im Lichte des 'Material Turn'. Edited by N. Weixlbaumer. *Anthologie zur Sozialgeographie. Abhandlungen zur Geographie und Regionalforschung*, Vol. 16, 83–105. Wien: IfGR.

Krieger, A. (2019). *City on a Hill. Urban Idealism in America from the Puritans to the Present.* Cambridge and London: The Belknap Press of Harvard University Press.

Latour, B. & Woolgar, S. (1986). *Laboratory Life: The Construction of Scientific Facts.* Princeton, NJ: Princeton University Press.

Law, J. & Hassard, J. (Eds.) (1999). *Actor Network Theory and After.* Oxford and Malden, MA: Blackwell Publishing.

Le Corbusier. (1987). *The City of To-morrow and Its Planning.* New York: Dover Publications, Inc.

Lefebvre, H. (2003). *The Urban Revolution.* Translated by Robert Bononno. Minneapolis, MN, and London: University of Minnesota Press.

Magnavita, N. & Tripepi, G. & Chiorri, C. (2021). Telecommuting, Off-Time Work, and Intrusive Leadership in Workers' Well-Being. *Environmental Research and Public Health*, 18(7).

Marquardt, N. (2016). Counting the Countless: Statistics on Homelessness and the Spatial Ontology of Political Numbers. *Environment and Planning D. Society and Space*, Vol. 34(2), 301–318.

Merrifield, A. (2012). The Urban Question under Planetary Urbanization. *International Journal of Urban and Regional Research*, Vol. 37(3), 909–922.

Merrifield, A. (2013). *The Politics of the Encounter: Urban Theory and Protest under Planetary Urbanization.* Athens and London: University of Georgia Press.

Merriman, P. (2012). *Mobility, Space and Culture.* London: Routledge.

Montoriol-Garriga, J. (2020). Second Homes in Spain: Seaside or Sierra? Barcelona: Caixa Bank Research. https://www.caixabankresearch.com/en/sector-analysis/real-estate/second-homes-spain-seaside-or-sierra

More, T. (2003). *Utopia.* London: Penguin Classics.

Newman, P. & Kenworthy, J.R. (1989). *Cities and Automobile Dependence: An International Sourcebook.* Aldershot, UK: Gower Technical.

Nietzsche, F. (1911). *Ecce Homo.* Edinburgh and London: Project Gutenberg.

Ntounis, N. & Kanellopoulou, E. (2017). Normalising Jurisdictional Heterotopias through Place Branding; The Cases of Christiania and Metelkova. *Environment and Planning A*, Vol. 49(10), 2223–2240.

Official Statistics of Finland (2019). Changes in marital status [e-publication]. ISSN=1797-643X. 02 2019 [referred: 14.5.2021]. Access method: http://www.stat.fi/til/ssaaty/2019/02/ssaaty_2019_02_2020-11-12_tie_001_en.html

Official Statistics of Finland (2020). Buildings and free-time residences [e-publication]. ISSN=1798-6796. 2020, Free-time Residences 2020. Helsinki: Statistics Finland [referred: 30.9.2021]. Access method: http://www.stat.fi/til/rakke/2020/rakke_2020_2021-05-27_kat_001_en.html

Okawa, Y. (2019) *The Memory Police.* Translated by Stephen Snyder. New York: Pantheon Books.

Orwell, G. (1945). *Animal Farm.* London: Secker and Warburg.

Owen, R. (1813). *A New View of Society, or Essays on the Principle of the Formation of the Human Character.* London: Cadell and Davies.

Perelman, C. & Olbrechts-Tyteca, L. (1971). *The New Rhetoric. A Treatise on Argumentation.* Nogtre Dame, IN: University of Notre Dame Press.

Petty, J. & Young, A. (2020). Visible Homelessness in a "Livable City": Municipal Responses to Homelessness in Melbourne. *American Journal of Economics and Sociology*, 79(2), 401–426.

Plato. (1921). *Cratulys in Plato in Twelve Volumes*, Vol. 12. Translated by Harold N. Fowler. Cambridge, MA: Harvard University Press; London: William Heinemann Ltd.

Popper, K.R. (1957). *The Poverty of Historicism*. London: Routledge.

Popper, K.R. (2011). *Open Society and Its Enemies*. London: Routledge.

Popper, K.R. (1975). *The Logic of Scientific Discovery*. London: Hutchinson & CO.

Roe, E. (1994). *Narrative Policy Analysis*. Durham, NC: Duke University Press.

Ruhle, S.A. & Süß, S. (2020). Presenteeism and Absenteeism at Work—an Analysis of Archetypes of Sickness Attendance Cultures. *Journal of Business and Psychology*, Vol. 35, 241–255.

Ryynänen, L. (2020). Oikeus urbaaniin? Tutkielma funktionalistisen kaupunkisuunnittelun kritiikistä. The School of Arts, Design and Architecture, Master's Thesis.

Saarikivi, J. (2021, August 7). Marginaaliin kirjoittajan muistolle. *Helsingin Sanomat*.

Sacco, P.L. & Ghirardi, S. & Tartari, M. & Trimarchi, M. (2019). Two Versions of Heterotopia: The Role of Art Practices in Participative Urban Renewal Processes. *Cities*, Vol. 89, 199–208.

Saldanha, A. (2008). Heterotopia and Structuralism. *Environment and Planning A*, Vol. 40, 2080–2096.

Sartre, J. (1992). *Being and Nothingness. A Phenomenological Essay on Ontology*. New York: Washington Square Press.

Scarantino, A. (2003). Affordances Explained. *Philosophy of Science*, Vol. 70, 949–961.

Schier, M. & Hilti, N. & Schad, H. & Tippel, C. & Dittrich-Wesbuer, A. & Monz, A. (2015). Residential Multi-Locality Studies – The Added Value for Research on Families and Second Homes. *Tijdschrift voor Economishe en Sociale Geografie*, Vol. 106(4), 439–452.

Schier, M. & Schlinzig, T. & Montanari, G. (2015). The Logic of Multi-Local Living Arrangements: Methodological Challenges and the Potential of Qualitative Approaches. *Tijdschrift voor Economishe en Sociale Geografie*, Vol. 106(4), 425–438.

Scarantino, A. (2003). Affordances Explained. *Philosophy of Science*, Vol. 70, 949–961.

Sharon, T. & Zandbergen, D. (2017). From Data Fetishism to Quantifying Selves: Self-Tracking Practices and the Other Values of Data. *New Media & Society*, Vol. 19(11), 1695–1709.

Shaw, D.B. (2018). *Posthuman Urbanism. Mapping Bodies in Contemporary City Space*. London & New York: Rowman & Littlefield.

Shaw, R.E. & Kinsella-Shaw, J.M. & Mice, W.M. (2019). Affordance Types and Affordance Tokens: Are Gibson's Affordances Trustworthy? *Ecological Psychology*, Vol. 31(1), DOI: 10.1080/10407413.2018.1508353.

Sorokowska, A. & Sorokowski, P. & Hilpert, P. & Cantarero, K., Frackowiak, T. & Ahmadi, K. & Alghraibeh, M., & Aryeetey, R. & Bertoni, A. & Bettache, K. et al. (2017). Preferred Interpersonal Distances: A Global Comparison. *Journal of Cross-Cultural Psychology*, Vol. 48(4), 577–592.

Stavrou, E.T. (2005). Flexible Work Bundles and Organizational Competitiveness: A Cross-national Study of the European Work Context. *Journal of Organizational Behavior*, Vol. 26, 923–947.

Strandell, A. (2017). Asukasbarometri 2016. Suomen ympäristökeskuksen raportteja, 19/2017.

Tuan, Y. (2011). *Space and Place. The Perspective of Experience.* Minneapolis and London: University of Minnesota Press.

Van Eemeren, F.H. & Grootendorst, R. & Snoeck Henkemans, F. (1996). *Fundamentals of Argumentation Theory. A Handbook of Historical Backgrounds and Contemporary Developments.* London: Routledge.

Voutilainen, O. & Korhonen, K. & Ovaskaja, O. & Vihinen, H. (2021). *Mökkibarometri. Luonnonvara- ja biotalouden tutkimus 47/21.* Helsinki: Luonnonvarakeskus.

Weichhart, P. (2015). Residential Multi-Locality: In Search of Theoretical Frameworks. *Tijdschrift voor Economische en Sociale Geografie*, Vol. 106(4), 378–391.

Weiske, C. & Petzold, K. & Schad, H. (2015). Multi-Local Living—The Approaches of Rational Choice Theory, Sociology of Everyday Life and Actor-Network Theory. *Tijdschrift voor Economishe en Sociale Geografie*, Vol. 106(4), 392–408.

Wittgenstein, L. (1922). *Tractatus Logico-Philosophicus.* New York: Kegan Paul, Trench & Co., Ltd, Harcourt, Brace & Company, Inc. Project Gutenberg.

United Nations. (2017). Principles and Recommendations for Population and Housing Censuses. Department of Economic and Social Affairs, Population Division, ST/ESA/STAT/SER.M/67/Rev.3.

United Nations (2019). World Population Prospects 2019: Highlights. Department of Economic and Social Affairs, Population Division, ST/ESA/SER.A/423.

Index